I0606350

Integrated Design
for a Sustainable Future

CONTENTS

FOREWORD

Ed Mazria **FAIA** Founder, Architecture 2030 | 2021 AIA Gold Medal Honoree

As the world grapples with the escalating realities of climate change, the role of architects, engineers, landscape architects, planners, and designers has never been more critical. This book, a testament to the transformative power of design, offers not just a vision for a sustainable future, but a tangible road map for achieving it. Within these pages, you will discover a compelling narrative of innovation and unwavering commitment to environmental stewardship.

At its core, this important book is a call to action—a reminder that the choices we make today will shape the world for generations to come. It is a declaration of accountability, optimism, and shared responsibility. The challenges facing our planet demand more than incremental change; they require a fundamental rethinking of how we design, build, and inhabit the spaces around us. This book not only outlines a path for this transformation but also demonstrates how these principles are already being applied.

In 2005, Architecture 2030 issued the 2030 Challenge, calling for incremental emissions reductions for all new buildings, developments, and major renovations to achieve carbon neutrality in 2030. To support this call to action, the American Institute of Architects (AIA) created the AIA 2030 Commitment in 2010, a national program structured to help firms meet and track progress toward meeting these targets.

LPA Design Studios, an integrated design firm of architects, engineers, interior designers, landscape architects, and researchers, was an early advocate and leader in the 2030 Commitment. They have demonstrated consistent success in achieving the Challenge targets across their entire portfolio of work.

The introduction sets the tone for the book: Nothing is too small to matter, and no challenge is insurmountable. The maxim "Every Project. Every Budget. Every Scale." embodies LPA's uncompromising commitment to environmental stewardship. Whether designing a modest school or a sprawling campus, every decision counts, and sustainability can always be integrated into the design process. But this is not a solitary endeavor. The firm emphasizes the importance of partnerships and collaboration, acknowledging that addressing climate change requires a collective effort, an integrated design team involving clients, architects, engineers, interior designers, landscape architects, researchers, and communities. This shared commitment empowers LPA to transcend individual limitations and achieve collective success.

LPA's dedication to informed design underscores their resolve to employ data-driven decision-making. By meticulously analyzing the impact of these decisions, they ensure that sustainability is not an afterthought, but an integral component of the design process. This research-driven approach allows them to seamlessly merge ambitious carbon-emission targets and environmental responsibility with the needs of their clients and the communities they serve, demonstrating that high-performance design is achievable across all project types, budgets, and scales. They prioritize firm-wide education, fostering the growth and development of emerging talent.

Beyond the theoretical framework, this book delves into the practical application of these principles through a diverse portfolio of projects. Each case study provides a compelling narrative of how LPA translates vision into reality, showcasing the tangible impact of their design approach. From transformative educational spaces that empower underserved communities to resilient housing solutions addressing the pressing need for affordable and sustainable living, these projects exemplify the power of design to effect positive change. A variety of other project types, including civic and commercial buildings that underscore how LPA's integrated design approach bridges aesthetics, performance, and purpose, proves that high-performance design is achievable across all scales and budgets. Together, these case studies illustrate how design can overcome constraints and deliver solutions that leave a legacy for both people and the environment.

In essence, this book is evidence of the power of design to shape a better future. It is a call to architects, planners, and all those involved in the built environment to embrace their role as catalysts for change. It challenges readers to reconsider what is possible in their own work and recognize the profound impact of thoughtful, informed design. Looking ahead, the principles and practices outlined in this book guide us toward a zero-carbon future, a future where environmental stewardship is not just a goal but a reality.

We're cutting carbon emissions

on every project,
for every budget,
at every scale.

And we're doing it like no one else.

No excuses.

WE BELIEVE

Everything counts.

We consistently hold ourselves accountable—to our clients, whose budgets we steward; to each other, in our commitment to partnership; and to the planet, because there is no time to waste.

There is always a way.

When design is informed by an integrated team, a sustainable solution is always possible. It's our job to translate that value to our clients.

We don't do this alone.

Addressing climate change demands collective effort. With our clients, our teammates, and our collaborators, we are developing a new model for the future.

PRACTICE

We lead with climate responsibility to make a difference.

From humble beginnings, we grew as a multidisciplinary design collective, united by a shared responsibility to drive down carbon emissions on every project, every budget, and every scale.

Early on, we decided as a firm to stake a claim that sustainable design is good design, and we set out to prove to our clients that a high-performance project doesn't have to cost more. For us, it didn't make sense to separate performance from beauty, occupant well-being, and the other elements that make a project a success.

When LEED was introduced in 2000, we enthusiastically embraced the idea of a universal rating system for green buildings and set out to see what we could do. We established several firsts, including the first LEED NC-certified building in the United States, the 325,000-square-foot Ford Premier Automotive Group headquarters. In 2004, we took it a step further and challenged ourselves to make every LPA project perform 25% better than California's Title 24, one of the toughest energy codes in the country. As the firm grew, we intentionally expanded to practice areas that were traditionally underserved by high-performance design—speculative office buildings, community colleges, public schools, and municipal buildings.

It's a marathon, not a sprint.

In ten years, we've shown that any firm, of any size, with any project mix, can make massive progress on carbon emissions. But progress is not a straight line up. 2023 was a wake-up call, and we've rebounded by doubling down on what made us successful: accountability, optimism, and shared responsibility.

AIA 2030 TARGETS

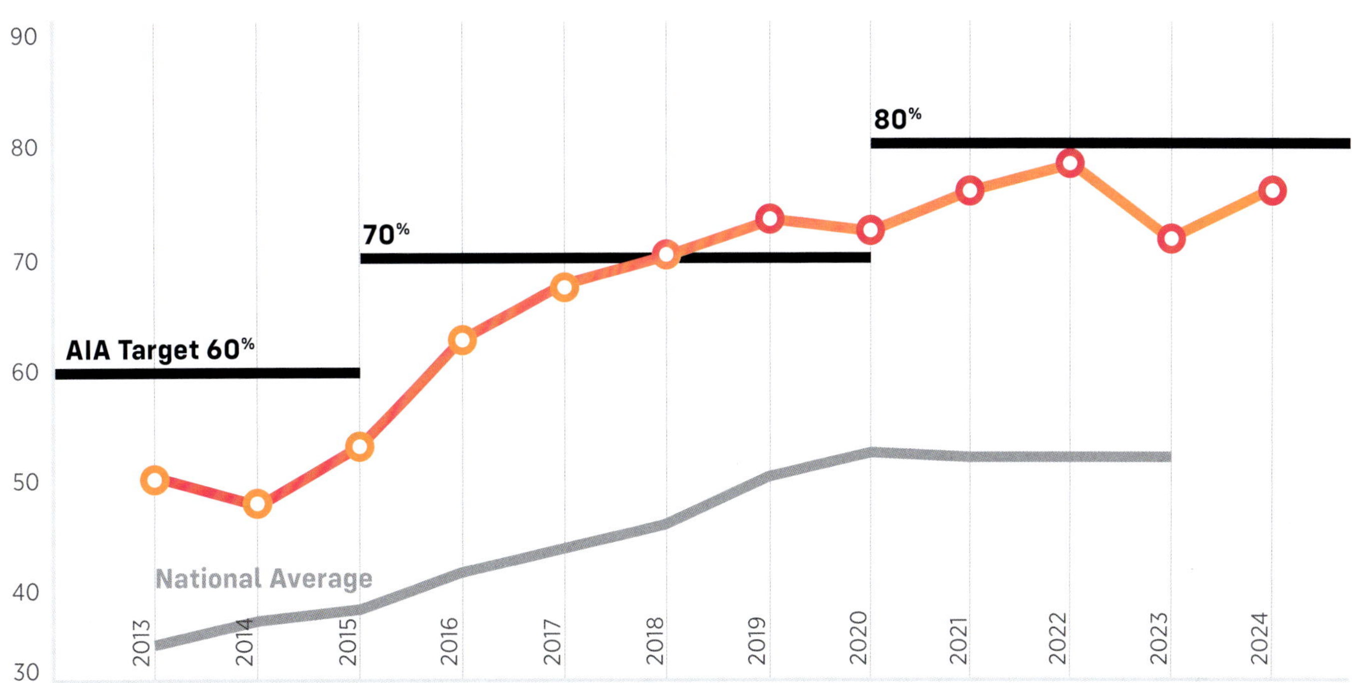

PREDICTED EUI REDUCTION

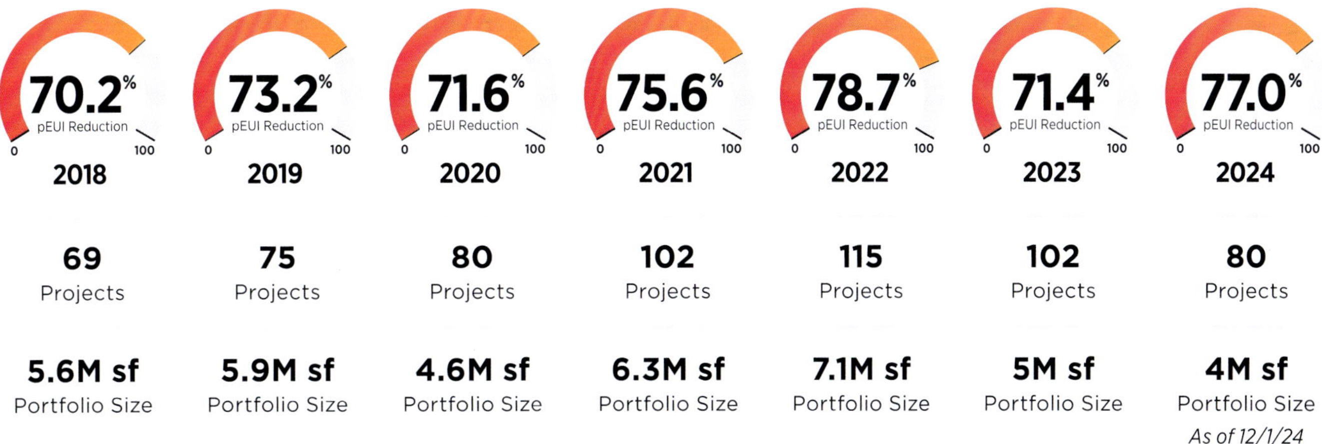

2018	2019	2020	2021	2022	2023	2024
69 Projects	**75** Projects	**80** Projects	**102** Projects	**115** Projects	**102** Projects	**80** Projects
5.6M sf Portfolio Size	**5.9M sf** Portfolio Size	**4.6M sf** Portfolio Size	**6.3M sf** Portfolio Size	**7.1M sf** Portfolio Size	**5M sf** Portfolio Size	**4M sf** Portfolio Size *As of 12/1/24*

Percentage of CO_2e Avoided

CO_2e Avoided

Baseline CO_2e

Project's Predicted CO_2e

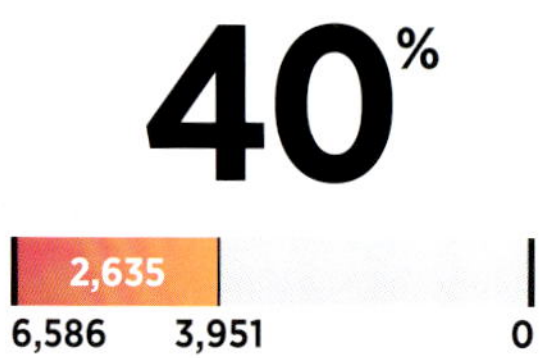

CARBON (CO_2e) **EMISSIONS AVOIDED**

(mT) Embodied Carbon

(mT/year) Operational Carbon

Percentage of pEUI Reduction

Baseline pEUI

Project's pEUI

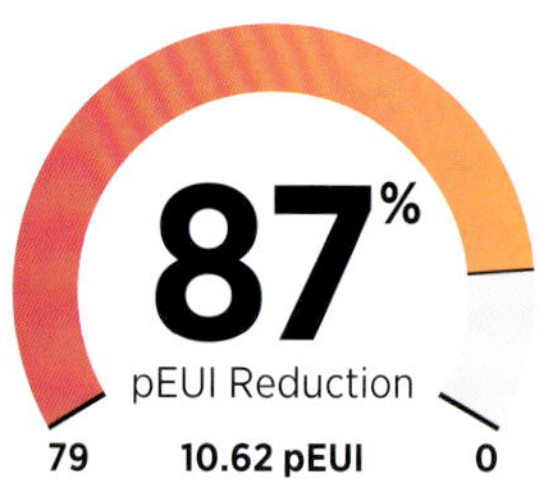

PREDICTED ENERGY USE INTENSITY (pEUI)

(kBtu/sf/year)

Met the AIA Commitment
80% THRESHOLD
at the time of design

"I hope LPA keeps dragging the rest of the industry along with them."

Ed Mazria **FAIA**, Founder, Architecture 2030

But it wasn't enough. Over the years, we reworked almost every element of how we practiced. We went from a traditional architectural firm to a fully integrated design studio built on common priorities and goals to make a difference. It started with interior designers and landscape architects, and by 2010 we had a full team in every engineering discipline. To deepen our rigor around evidence-based design, human health, and community engagement, we established our applied research group, giving us the foundation for an informed design approach.

To bust the status quo, we knew we had to work together differently. We structured the firm to erase hierarchies between disciplines and remove boundaries to collaboration, regardless of the makeup of the team. We made the AIA 2030 Commitment targets our targets, and we integrated the AIA Framework for Design Excellence into every discipline to set measurable goals for performance, community, wellness, and experience.

As we learned, we grew as a team. "Doing more with less" became our mantra. We embraced the best evaluative tools available, from early-phase pEUI calculators to embodied carbon—and committed to publishing our results. We learned to position our ecological goals in terms of the client's goals and budget. We sweated every detail.

LPA'S LEADERSHIP TEAM built the firm around inclusivity, diversity, and a commitment to deliver more for clients.

Our success is measured in different ways. For six years we maintained an average of 73.5% pEUI reduction across 34.5 million square feet, exceeding the national average established by 2030 Commitment reporting firms by 50%. Our projects earned national awards from architecture, engineering, landscape architects, and design groups as we set new benchmarks for building performance and transparency. And, most important, we earned the trust of our clients and communities and made them sustainability champions. Our leaders have become industry leaders.

At the same time, we've developed a new model for architectural practice built on a foundation of informed design, integrated teams, research, and culture. We've shown what is possible. Sustainable design is no longer only reserved for high-budget, mission-driven projects. Our industry must confront climate change.

No excuses.

NO MORE BUSINESS AS USUAL.

Dan Heinfeld **FAIA**
President, LPA Design Studios
(1986–2023)

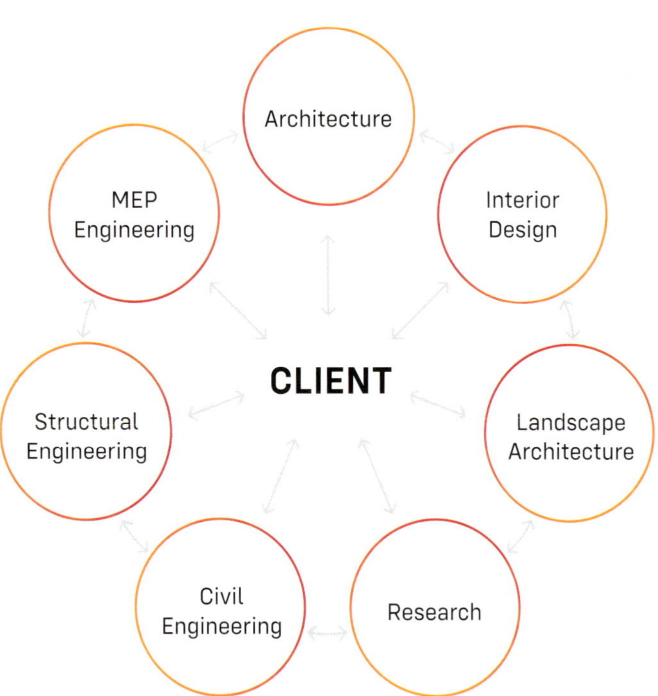

In its early years, LPA followed the traditional model for an architecture firm. When we were hired for a project, we contracted with outside consultants to provide landscape and engineering services. These teams often varied from project to project, reflecting different skills, relationships, and corporate interests. Most of the time, they behaved like consultants—they were not fully invested in the success of the project. Rarely were they truly part of the team; they didn't share the same culture, principles, or willingness to tackle the complex challenges of creating sustainable, high-performance buildings.

As LPA started to grow, we became increasingly frustrated by this process. Our buildings succeeded on many levels, but we knew we could do better. As energy costs soared and climate change became a real issue, we knew we wouldn't achieve any meaningful impact if we continued to practice in the same way as architects had been practicing for decades.

That realization was the start of a thirty-year effort to fundamentally change our approach to design. As a firm, we committed to rethinking the traditional concepts. We set out to develop a practice based on the idea that design excellence and high performance were the same thing. You couldn't have one without the other. A beautiful project should also be a sustainable, resilient building, or you couldn't call it a success.

Over the years, we reworked almost every element of how we practiced. We went from a traditional architectural firm to a fully integrated design studio—with engineers, landscape architects, and interior designers working in-house—focused on creating a more collaborative design environment around common priorities and goals. The idea of an integrated design firm wasn't new, but it was still a rarity. Architects and engineers liked to stay in their lanes. But we found people in different disciplines who wanted a seat at the table and the opportunity to play a greater role in projects. They wanted to influence projects in a way that they couldn't at a traditional engineering or landscape architecture firm.

This collective vision and shared process profoundly changed the firm. With the addition of each new discipline, a culture of sharing evolved. The synergies between the disciplines grew, as did engagement. Architectural teams and our in-house engineers, interior designers, and landscape architects began to collaborate at the beginning of the process with the knowledge that a better process creates better results. The barriers of fee and scope were removed, giving our clients easy access to all the disciplines, when needed.

As we evolved and learned, we saw the difference in our projects. Communities were engaged and responsive to the process. Our buildings performed better. We were able to reduce energy use, cut operating costs, and design buildings that worked for people and the environment. Year after year, we posted nation-leading energy performance numbers, hitting targets many believed couldn't be met by a large firm working across market sectors.

We knew integration would make us a better sustainable firm, but it also made us better architects, designers, and engineers. Working together inherently made us look at the world in a different way. A building is like an organic system. If you push here, it pulls something there. You take away here, it adds there. It's this interplay between all these things. And if you address that right, you'll practice differently.

Through the process, we developed a shared attitude: no excuses. As architects, engineers, and designers, we can't control everything. But we can influence the context and the response, and the building performance. We have a unique seat at the table to create something beautiful and sustainable, where performance and design excellence coexist. We're the ones who can lead and make a difference. Our work demonstrates that an integrated design firm can be an agent of change.

THE PREMIER AUTOMOTIVE GROUP headquarters in Irvine, California, was the first LEED NCv2.0-certified building in the United States.

Becoming LPA

The inflection points in our history showed us new ways of working together, shaped our process, and became embedded in our culture.

1990

IRVINE RANCH WATER DISTRICT

Ten years before LEED, this AIA Test of Time winner embodied all ten Framework for Design Excellence measures.

2003

TOYOTA MOTOR SALES, SOUTH CAMPUS

The *New York Times* called it proof that sustainable design could be achieved under a standard developer budget.

1965

LPA FOUNDED IN ORANGE, CA

1971

FIRST AIA DESIGN AWARD

1996

DEVELOPED FIRM MISSION & VALUES

2001

FIRST LEED PROJECT

2004

FIRST FIRMWIDE ENERGY TARGETS

2005

ESTABLISHED LEED TRAINING

2008

SAVINGS BY DESIGN

2009

LPA UNIVERSITY (LPA+U)

2010

PROFESSIONAL DEVELOPMENT GRANTS

1965 2000 2005 2010

2013

CSUN STUDENT RECREATION CENTER

After onboarding mechanical engineering, our integrated teams were galvanized by this collaboration.

2014

COASTLINE COMMUNITY COLLEGE, NEWPORT

Before our models could deal with natural ventilation, this passively cooled campus demonstrated its energy impact.

2024

HOAG HOSPITAL, IRVINE

Our next horizon is healthcare, as we set out to change how this energy-hungry typology treats the environment.

2011

2030 COMMITMENT SIGNATORY

2013

FIRST YEAR REPORTING 2030 COMMITMENT

2015

ESTABLISHED LPA 4 CHANGE

2016

EMBARK PROGRAM FOR INTERNS & NEW GRADS

CAREER DEVELOPMENT PATH

2018

BALANCE PROGRAM

MET THE 2030 COMMITMENT 70% THRESHOLD FOR THE FIRST TIME

2020

AIA COTE TOP TEN+ AWARD

ENGAGEMENT / CLIFTON STRENGTHS

PROFESSIONAL DEVELOPMENT PLAN

FOUNDED EDI COMMITTEE

DIVERSITY IN DESIGN SCHOLARSHIP

2022

PATHFINDER INTERN PROGRAM

2023

AIA ARCHITECTURE AWARD

ALTERNATE CAREER PATH

2025

AIA ARCHITECTURE FIRM AWARD

2015

2020

2025

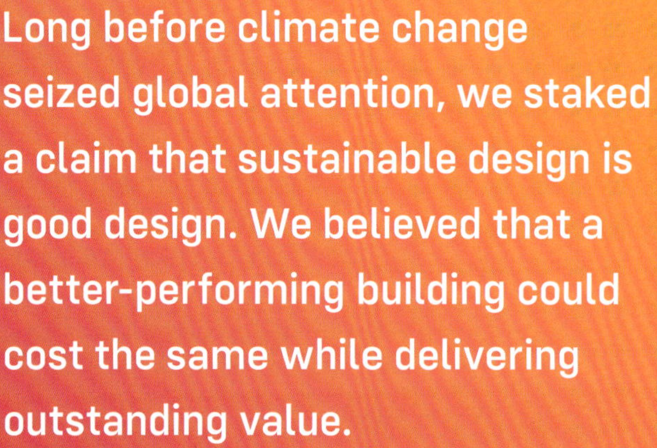

Long before climate change seized global attention, we staked a claim that sustainable design is good design. We believed that a better-performing building could cost the same while delivering outstanding value.

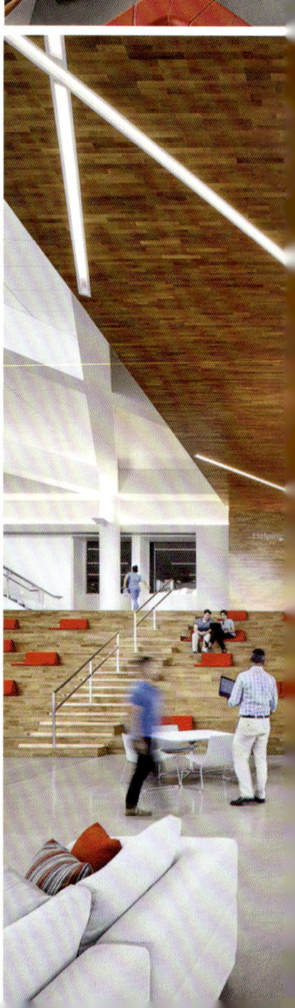

We embrace integrated teams to achieve our goals.

Significant carbon reduction demands the attention of every discipline, working as a team. The partnership among disciplines shapes everything we do.

Integrated teams, working as a collective unit, help us to better understand the impact of our decisions and to ask better questions. Our culture focuses on removing barriers, with architects, landscape architects, interior designers, and engineers sharing a creative table from the start.

Disciplines aren't divided into business groups or in competition with external consultants. Studios are not "profit centers." Our core business and creative unit is the firmwide integrated team, operating under a common client contract, free from fee splits, aligned toward common goals. When we work with outside experts, they follow the same principles. The mindset is the same for every project.

UNLOCKING INNOVATION

Our collective approach finds innovations that aren't possible on a traditional team. We've found cross-pollination generates stronger ideas. Every voice is heard. When every discipline is fully invested from the very beginning, the initial spark of a concept is protected to the very end.

A GALVANIZING MOMENT HAPPENED IN 2008, when we designed the campus recreation center at CSU Northridge. On a narrow site with poor solar orientation, the structural, mechanical, electrical, and architectural leads collaborated to seamlessly integrate displacement ventilation, optimize the structure, and reduce solar gain. As each design idea cascaded into the next, a section emerged that no one discipline could have conceived alone. The experience showed us what was possible when individual talents merge into one team.

CSU NORTHRIDGE STUDENT RECREATION CENTER: INTEGRATED SECTION

The Fold

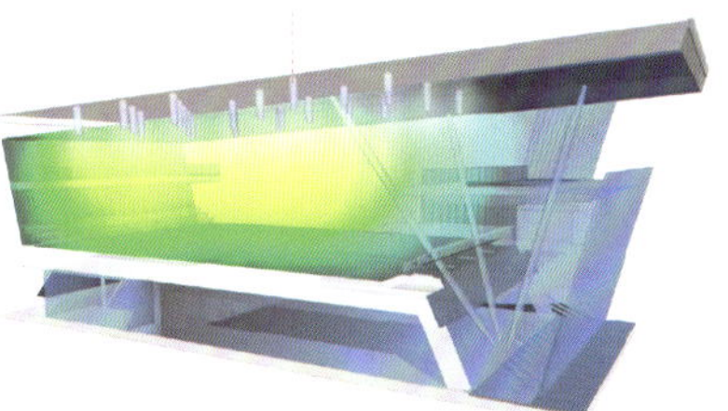

Natural Light

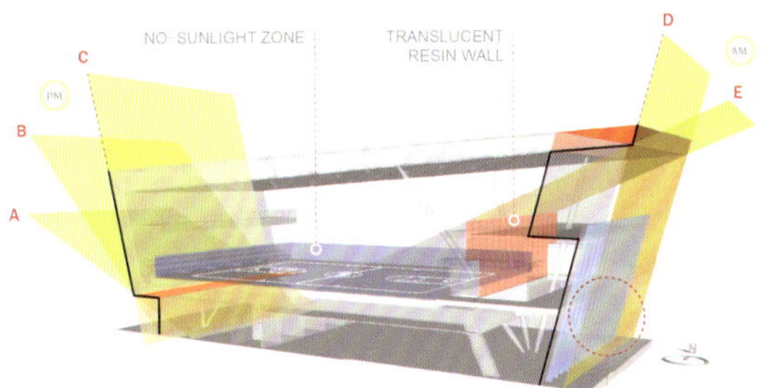

Shade Fin Glass Coverage

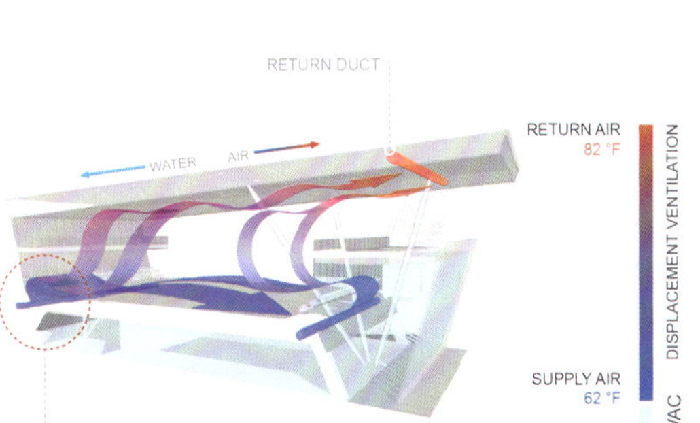

Hybrid Ventilation System

OUR INTEGRATED TEAMS MAKE SPACE FOR NEW IDEAS and alternative view-points. For the net-zero-energy Starr Atrium on Edwards Lifesciences' Irvine, California, campus, a structural engineer's "inspired idea" for a structural "net" to span the large, open atrium resulted in an iconic effect, dazzling with its play of light and shadow beneath the skylight.

TEACHING DESIGN EMPATHY

This partnership mentality isn't taught in schools; we had to cultivate it. We teach design empathy. Our Integrated Design Residency is a ten-month program where designers switch roles with another discipline and experience every phase of a project in a colleague's shoes. Our Integrated Design Playbook was created as a road map for inclusion and helping teams understand every member's roles, gifts, and challenges.

TOWARD INFORMED DESIGN

We embraced integrated teams to better understand the impact of our decisions and to help our clients to ask better questions, resulting in high-performance projects that meet their goals and add tremendous value.

We are better together.

SHAPING THE PROFESSION

Changing an industry involves the whole industry. We advocate for integrated, informed design, not to win work but to spread a model of architectural practice that is critically important for our shared future. Every time we publish, speak, partner, or serve, we are moving the conversation from inside LPA into the industry.

"LPA's integrated design team of architects, engineers, interior designers, and landscape architects was essential in achieving our aggressive performance goals on campus. LPA's in-house services made a believer of me that this kind of integration is truly better."

Tom Porter, Senior Vice President
Corporate Services, Edwards Lifesciences

Informed design grounds our work and maximizes our impact.

Informed design—our research-driven approach—turns our passion for sustainability into value for clients. Understanding the impact of design decisions allows us to merge carbon emissions targets with the project goals. It's the recipe for high performance.

"The Living Building Challenge is called 'challenge' for a reason. The Environmental Nature Center was only the third project in Southern California to earn Petal Certification, a standard that requires a multidiscipline approach to design facilities that restore and support the local community."

Lindsay Baker, CEO, International Living Future Institute

Early in LPA's history, we followed a simple rule: "Every building should know where the sun is." When performance analysis modeling emerged, we recognized the power of modeling to maximize energy performance when used strategically and consistently. Paired with a focus on budget stewardship, we arrived at a process that is data-driven but not prescriptive; process-oriented but still fluid and responsive. We measure the performance of our informed design approach in three ways.

BUDGET PERFORMANCE

We make the best use of clients' budgets by making high-performance design an intrinsic aspect of every project. Sustainability isn't an add-on. It's baked in. Clients don't pay extra for sustainable design.

WHEN SANTIAGO CANYON COLLEGE LAUNCHED a new humanities building, it was uninterested in LEED certification. Budget was everything. Five years later, when priorities changed, they asked what upgrades would be needed to qualify for certification. None, it turned out. The building was already eligible for LEED Gold certification.

ON EDUCATION PROJECTS, SUSTAINABILITY CAN ALWAYS ADD VALUE as a teaching tool. For Tarbut V'Torah Day School campus in Irvine, California, stormwater is interwoven with the educational and architectural goals.

ENVIRONMENTAL PERFORMANCE

On every project, we take a "passive first" approach, emphasizing free or inexpensive solutions before turning to high-tech load-reduction strategies and renewables. Modeling plays a role from the earliest stages, helping us validate decisions and wring every bit of efficiency from the design.

PROGRAM PERFORMANCE

No space is wasted, every design decision serves multiple purposes, and every aspect works in harmony. We are meticulous about understanding the needs of communities and finding unexpected ways to delight, serve, and empower.

Informed design is a pathway to a deep connection between the environment and the people who use our spaces. At a fundamental level, a building that "always knows where the sun is" taps into something universal and profound, changing lives by design.

Spectrum IV in San Diego reflects the humanity embedded in sustainable design. Situated on a canyon's edge, the lab building brings researchers in touch with moments of intuition and discovery. Perforated sunshades and fritted glass filter dappled light into every lab and office without obstructing the rugged landscape. Each facade bears the signature of sun patterns that will outlast all of us.

Informed design is not just "by the numbers." It's about making better decisions to deliver beautiful outcomes.

"LPA is demonstrating that it is possible for us to achieve our performance goals. Their willingness to share their results and best practices is pushing us all to up our game."

Ted Hyman **FAIA**, Managing Partner, ZGF

We use applied research to understand the impact of our work and push further.

Informed design is only possible when research is embedded throughout the process. In our drive for continuous improvement, teams persistently push for data to validate performance decisions.

Our Sustainability + Applied Research (S+AR) team brings designers the tools, resources, and hands-on training needed to understand complex issues, formulate informed options, and help our clients make smart decisions. This team of performance modelers, environmental psychologists, and health and materials specialists brings academic rigor to our sustainability goals.

Our Research Process

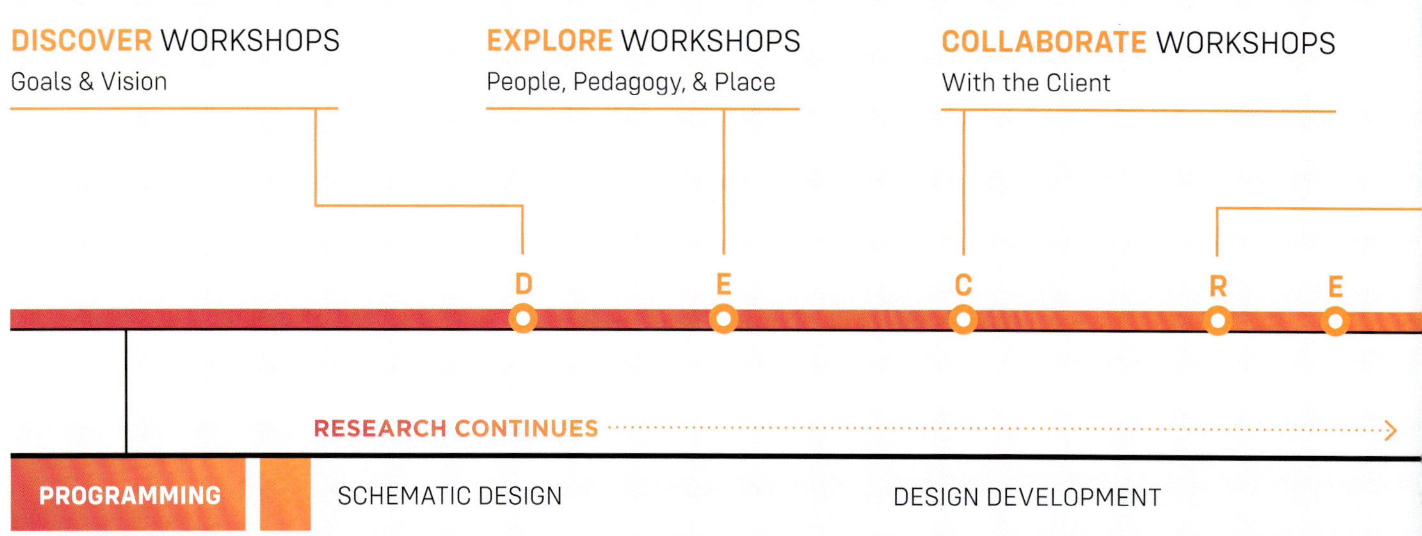

ON THE UNDER-CONSTRUCTION HOAG HOSPITAL IRVINE EXPANSION, the stamp of the research effort can be found throughout the facility, which is designed to prioritize specialized care, connections to nature, and a comprehensive patient experience.

EMPHASIS ON "APPLIED"

Serving as a resource to our project teams, the S+AR team applies their skills throughout the design process—distilling existing knowledge, collecting and analyzing community input, conducting carbon analyses, advising on certifications, and conducting pre- and post-occupancy evaluations. Over the last ten years, S+AR has produced research briefs on dozens of topics, contributing to widespread implementation of active design, biophilia, infection control, school safety, embodied carbon reduction, neurodiversity accommodation, and mass timber in our projects.

CODIFYING OUR APPROACH

Academic partnerships are critical to our research approach and understanding of evidence-based design. We developed our sustainability benchmarking approach in collaboration with teams from the University of California, Irvine and University of California, San Diego. With UC Berkeley's Center

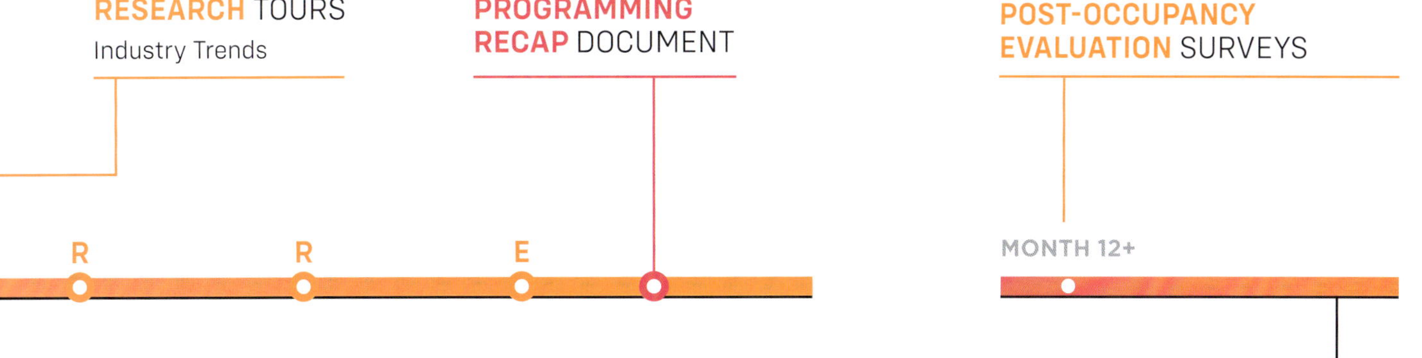

FAST COMPANY

2024

BEST WORKPLACES FOR INNOVATORS AWARD

for the Built Environment, we integrated post-occupancy evaluations. And working with UC San Diego's Mobile Technology Learning Center (MTLC), we bridged the gap between education research and innovative learning spaces.

The AIA Framework for Design Excellence provides the foundation for our four pillars of sustainability: performance, community, wellness, and experience. Instead of a checklist approach, the framework provides a simple goal-setting tool that is compelling to clients regardless of their attitudes toward sustainability.

ETHICAL ENGAGEMENT

S+AR researchers work with design to craft community engagement plans to produce deep and meaningful responses and ensure everyone is represented. There are no boilerplates or templates. The outreach process is customized for each project, with the clear intent of developing community authorship.

Data and consistent, ongoing dialogue build trust and enable teams to design *with* the stakeholders, not *for* them. Everyone has a voice and a transparent view of the discussion. At the end of the day, research is a form of deep listening. And listening is the heart of design.

LPA RESEARCHERS AND DESIGNERS CREATED THE GOAL SETTING CARD DECK, a set of eighty cards developed to gamify the process of setting sustainable goals. Designers use the cards to take stakeholders through a carefully organized series of activities using a game board and other tactile elements. The deck has transformed sustainable design discussions, making them more accessible to diverse user groups.

FOR THE eSTEM CAMPUS, RESEARCHERS were embedded from the beginning, leading workshops and facility tours, modeling wind and sun conditions, training educators on their new spaces, and studying utilization of the finished building.

On every project, design teams develop project goals in four key areas: performance, wellness, experience, and community. The goals must be appropriate to the project, established in a dialogue with clients, informed by research, revisited throughout the design process, and evaluated post-occupancy.

WELLNESS

Sustain and enhance the mental and physical health of occupants.

EXPERIENCE

Elevate the spirit through strategies that produce delight, belonging, and collaboration.

PERFORMANCE

Protect our planet by minimizing energy, water, carbon emissions, and any other quantifiable metric.

COMMUNITY

Build strong, resilient communities within and beyond the project site.

It takes real investment to build a culture where every individual on every team sees the vision and has the skills and motivation to achieve it.

LPA
LPA

Our shared culture makes it possible.

What we're striving for isn't easy. Who we are. How we work together. How we grow to better serve our clients and communities. That's how we find success.

"Working with LPA is different. They engage all parties early, when they can really make a difference, and are relentless in their efforts to make sure every voice is heard."

Dennis Berkshire, President, ADG

Every voice counts. We check our egos at the door and work as teammates, wearing the same jersey, sharing the same values. Individually, we are architects, engineers, landscape architects, interior designers, and researchers. Together, we transcend what any of us could achieve on our own.

Our culture is grounded in shared responsibility. There is no "green team." Everyone owns sustainability. To support this, we maintain internal institutions and embrace industry frameworks that bring us together and keep us aligned. Our culture isn't just a set of values; it's an accelerator for transformation. It's what enables us to defy the odds, push boundaries, and ultimately deliver superior building performance.

CONTINUOUS LEARNING

Education is the heartbeat of our practice. A constant flow of reinforcing messages and information feeds our institutional memory.

We grow through monthly Sustainability Sessions and TechTalks, part of LPA+U, an evolving body of AIA-credentialed continuing education courses live-streamed and available on-demand. Quarterly Master Classes provide in-depth training. And an ecosystem of summits, residencies, and leadership programs helps us accelerate our evolution year over year.

DEFINING EXCELLENCE

Our process sets goals and measures success around four areas that take a broad view of sustainability—performance, experience, community, and wellness. Meeting the AIA 2030 Commitment is our performance benchmark on every project. Design teams use the AIA Framework for Design Excellence to solve for better health, wellness, and environmental outcomes. Every project we publish externally is accompanied by a graphic showcasing its performance across a broad set of metrics, good or bad.

AT MONTGOMERY MIDDLE SCHOOL IN SAN DIEGO, designers were the translators between the superintendent's bold vision for LEED Platinum and the facilities director's practical focus on simple systems.

PLAYBOOKS

Integrated Teams Playbook

Our manual for behaving like a deeply integrated team, the playbook outlines each team member's role, how they collaborate, and critical questions to ask.

Collaborative Planning

Our version of "pull planning," this Mural-based ecosystem provides a project delivery workflow in reverse, starting with performance outcomes and reverse engineering the steps to get there.

Sustainability Action Plan

Our Sustainability Action Plan offers a holistic vision and road map toward carbon neutrality.

TRANSLATING VALUE

Helping skeptical, budget-conscious clients understand the benefits of high-performance design is foundational to our work. It has led us to a process that accommodates every client's needs and aligns the client's values with sustainable design. Everyone on the team is expected to be fluent in life-cycle cost, initial investment versus long-term savings, and maintenance to make the business case for better-performing projects. If we are to succeed, we must be fierce protectors of our clients' budgets and vision.

LEADERS BUILDING LEADERS

As we've grown, we've made intentional moves to embrace hard conversations and create a culture of empowerment to increase representation at every level and ensure pay equity.

LPA leaders are active mentors, preparing future generations to lead the firm forward. From the beginning of every LPA employee's career, they become part of succession planning for intergenerational leadership. Our investments in professional development and flexible career paths are designed to support every professional in developing their strengths, finding their place, and reaching their highest potential.

STRENGTH THROUGH DIVERSITY

Our success as a firm depends on the diversity of perspectives we bring to our clients' challenges. We recognize the need for a stronger pipeline for underrepresented voices to enter the industry and become firm leaders. Data drives our approach. Since 2020, our Equity Diversity and Inclusion Advisory Council has worked with our S+AR group to benchmark our performance on employee diversity and pay equity and collect insights on our employees' personal experiences. Through the EDI Council and their annual report, we've seen our data-driven approach blossom into people-driven culture change.

GROWING TOGETHER

We are fierce and fluent advocates for sustainable design, ready to share authorship and work together for a higher purpose. Our challenge is to produce results at scale, and to build a culture where every individual on every team sees the vision and has the skills and motivation to achieve it. Our work proves that net zero is accessible to everyone. And in the big picture, it demonstrates that our industry can confront climate change.

No excuses.

EAGLE PASS, where the design director called every HVAC repair tech in the small border town to secure maintenance contracts for the VRF system. It was all-hands-on-deck to achieve the city's first all-electric facility.

PORTFOLIO

Transformative Experience

To shape high-performance projects that people will fight to preserve, they need to provide transformative experiences. These are places where people feel they belong; that spark pride and affection; that become part of the fabric of their communities.

TIDE Academy

A public Silicon Valley STEAM school levels the playing field.

Down the street from some of the biggest innovators in tech, a public STEAM school combats inequality by building a career pipeline for underserved students.

Sequoia Union High School District | Menlo Park, CA

> "The building is a statement, and its bold notion of programming provides students with a variety of unique spaces. It takes advantage of the climate and utilizes the outdoor spaces as learning environments."
>
> AIA CAE Jury

CONTEXT

In the increasingly privatized educational landscape of Silicon Valley, minority and disadvantaged students are excluded from the same tech industry boom that is actively pushing them out of their neighborhoods. In a bid to compete and do better for the 75% minority, 47% economically disadvantaged community, Sequoia Union High School District envisioned a STEAM program that would give public school students access to the same educational experiences and connections to academia and local business as private school students. Situated on a two-acre site four blocks from Meta, TIDE Academy is designed to prepare students for the kind of creative, collaborative, self-directed work accomplished just down the street.

OUTCOME

With a focus on inquiry-based learning and interdisciplinary instruction, TIDE mirrors the innovative environments graduates will encounter in future tech professions. Three buildings of studios and STEAM labs are organized in a C shape, protecting a plaza that functions as an outdoor multipurpose room. Taking advantage of the mild San Francisco Bay climate, much of the program was pushed outside to a network of collab and "think tank" spaces connected on three levels. As indoors and outdoors blend, the campus fosters a level of familiarity for the four-hundred-person student body, with spaces everywhere to socialize, perform, debate, and play. The design supports coming together and getting away, messy creativity and intense focus, creating students who are independent but know how to collaborate.

S.T.E.A.M. ON DISPLAY

OUTWARDLY FOCUSED TO INVITE INDUSTRY

Exposed to the busy street that houses some of the most innovative companies in the world, the design both protects and beckons.

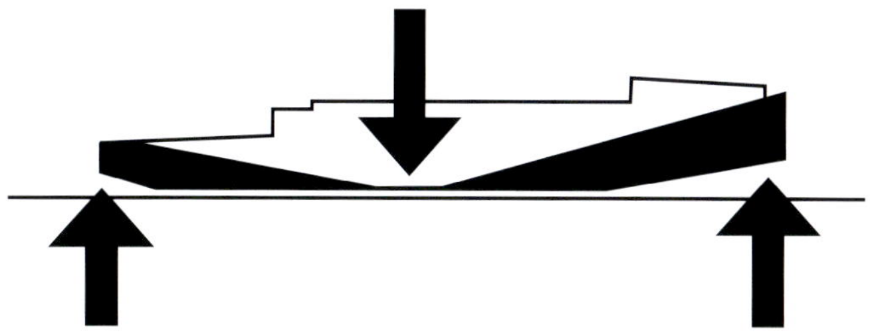

INTEGRATION

On the tight site, discussions across disciplines focused on activating every possible space around the district's collaborative goals. Landscape architects were active participants in discussions with educators, looking for opportunities to seamlessly blend indoor and outdoor learning environments. No space was wasted. Every floor was embedded with green spaces and planting areas. In total, seventeen distinct outdoor learning, collaboration, and gathering zones were developed for brainstorming or experiments, encouraging cross-collaboration, exploration, and creativity. To fit the pieces together, designers and landscape architects developed a flow to the exterior circulation and green spaces, bringing activity and movement to the vertical campus. A grand staircase with decks connects the different levels to the central courtyard, the heart of the campus, with interactive "huddle" spaces, social areas, and zones for students to find their own spots.

The lighting design blends and highlights the spaces, creating a sense that the interior learning environments flow into the open spaces and the central "oasis." A tall event pole with adjustable fixture heads was integrated into the outdoor plaza, providing broad illumination across the courtyard without using precious space. Recessed fixtures and lighting integrated into the handrails help wayfinding and define spaces. At night, in the transitioning industrial neighborhood, the exterior lighting organizes bright and dark environments to create a glowing hub in the community.

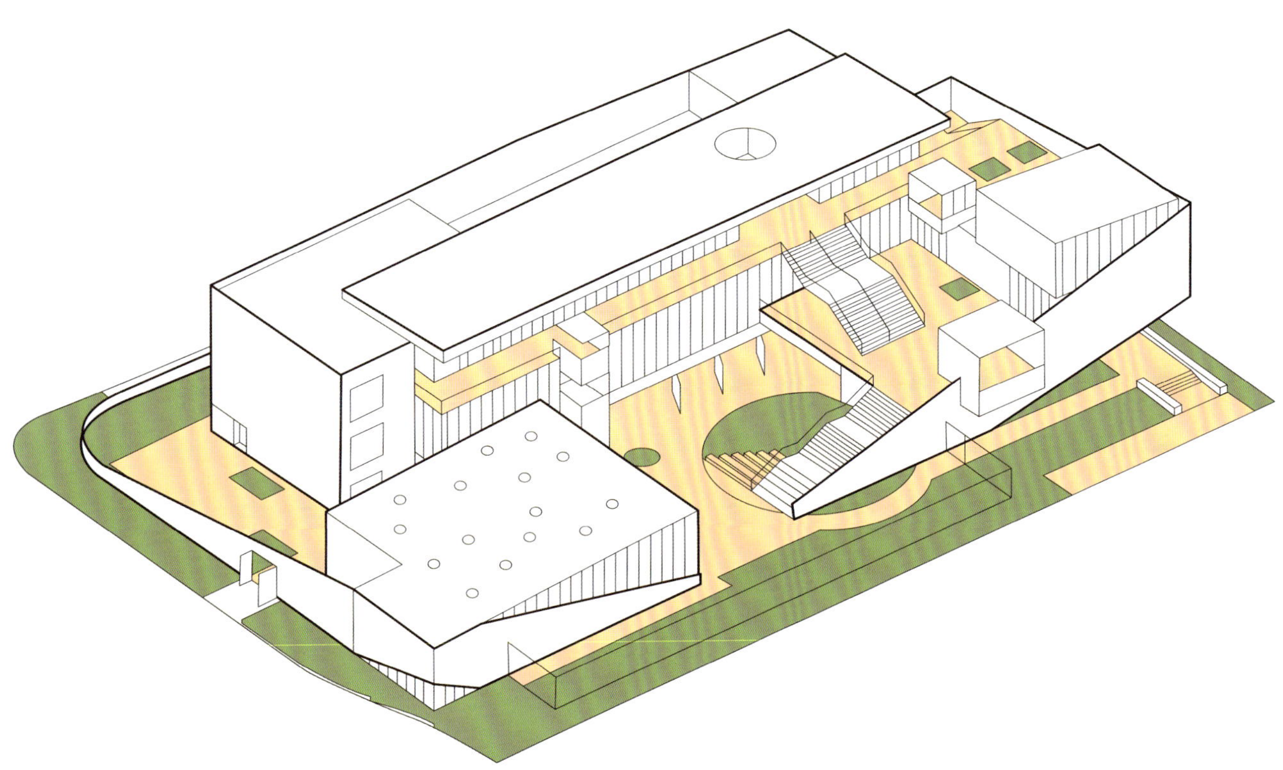

LANDSCAPE

NATURE AND GREEN SPACES WERE DESIGNED INTO EVERY LEVEL, HELPING TO CREATE AN ORGANIC, ACTIVE FLOW TO CAMPUS CIRCULATION ON THE TIGHT SITE.

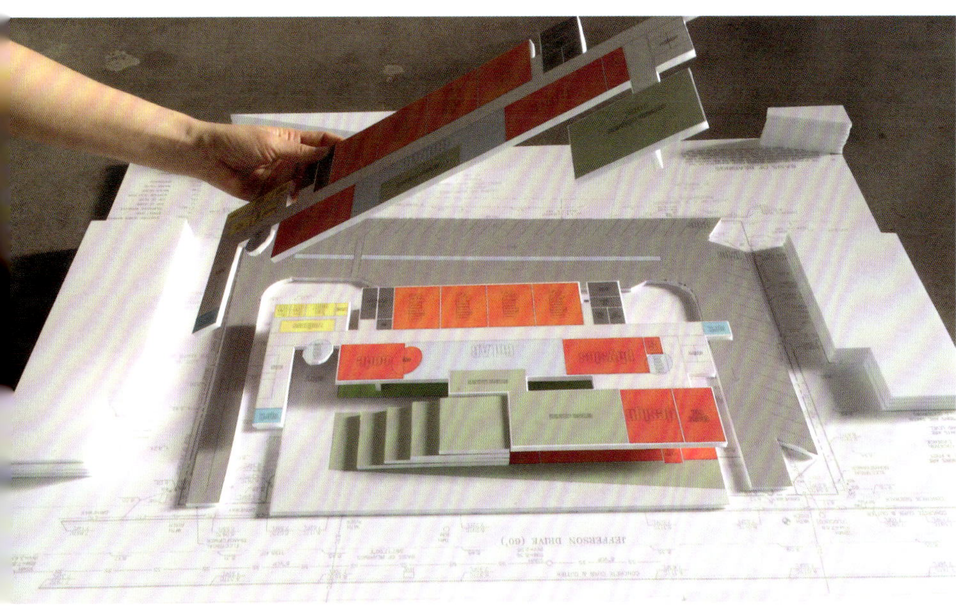

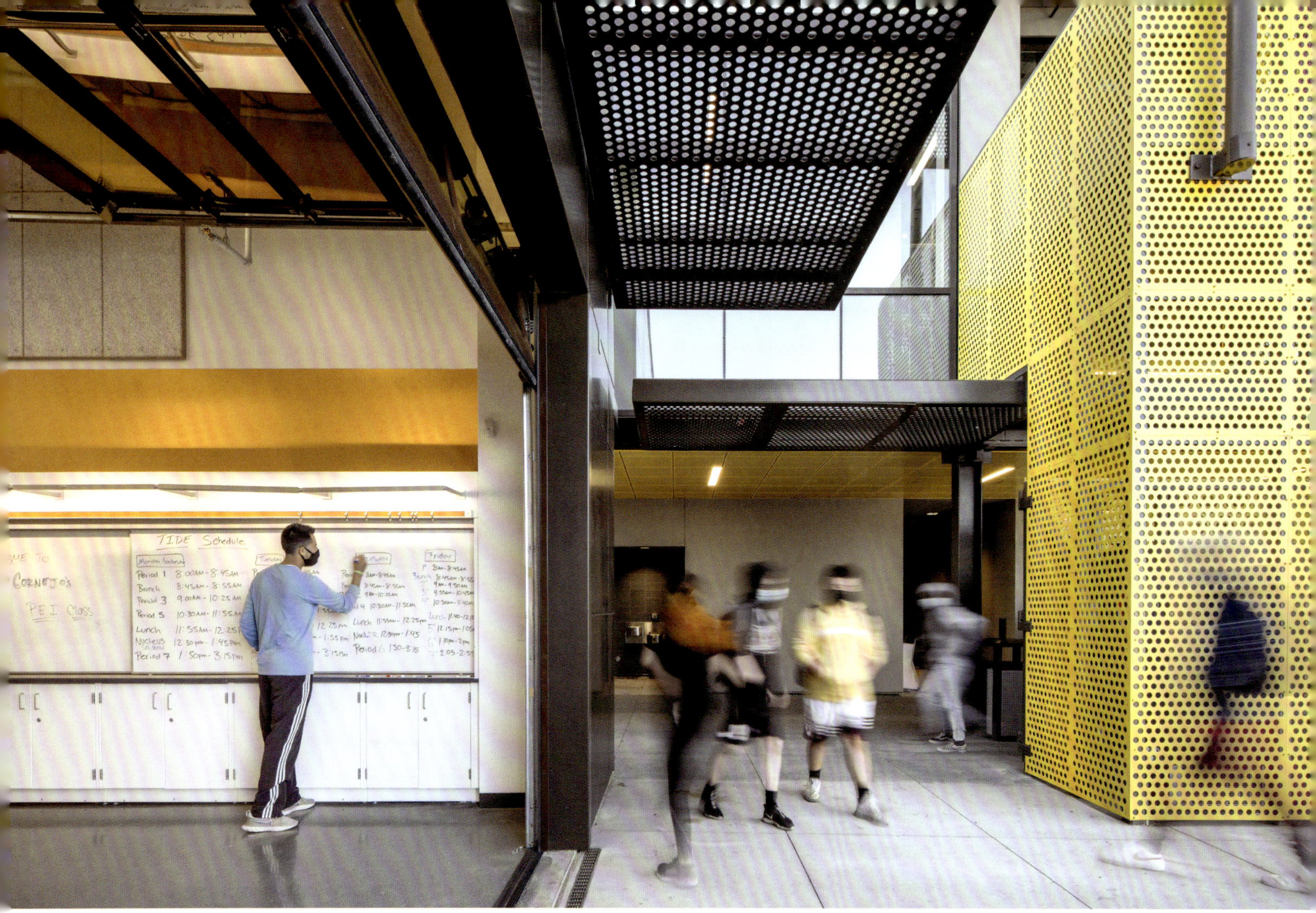

FRAMEWORK FOR DESIGN EXCELLENCE

DESIGN FOR INTEGRATION

Located on a two-acre site, the campus is open despite its density, with a protective U shape that opens out toward the street and puts education on display.

DESIGN FOR EQUITABLE COMMUNITIES

Serving disadvantaged students in an affluent city, TIDE evens access to high-quality STEAM environments.

DESIGN FOR ECONOMY

Without budget or space for a gym, fields, library, or student parking lot, TIDE utilizes civic amenities and makes the city an extension of the campus.

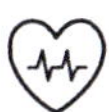

DESIGN FOR WELL-BEING

Diversity of space gives students control over their environment—from focused, to social, to alone-together. And 70% of learning spaces directly connect to the outdoors.

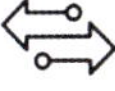

DESIGN FOR CHANGE

On a site three feet below sea level, a block away from the San Francisco Bay, the campus was elevated six feet to anticipate sea level rise.

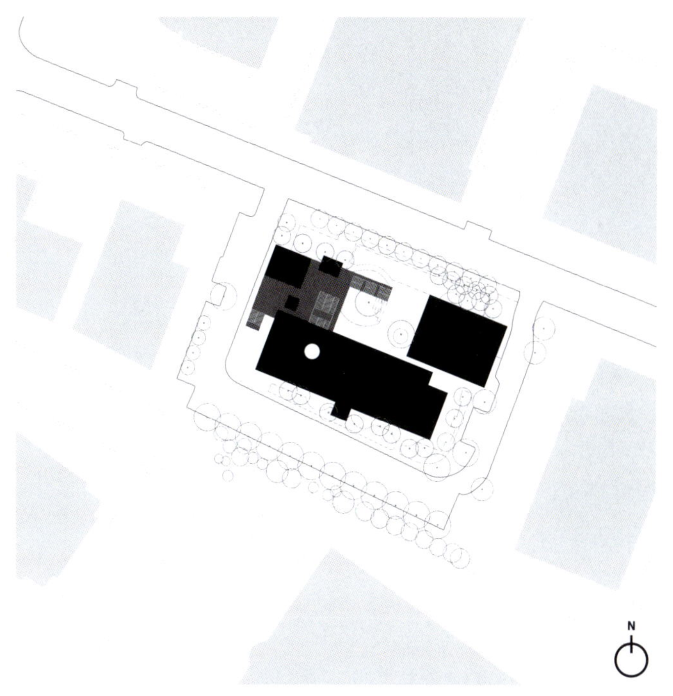

Performance

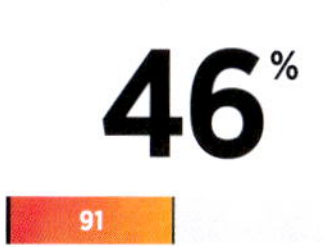

OPERATIONAL CARBON EMISSIONS AVOIDED (mT/year)

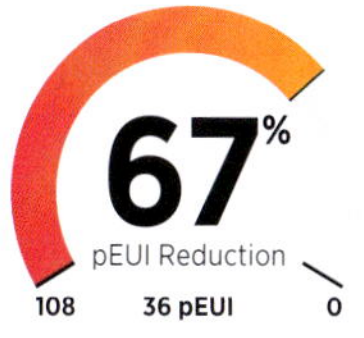

PREDICTED ENERGY USE INTENSITY (kBtu/sf/year)

Project	K-12 | Public | 2019
Budget	$29 M
Scale	Small | 44,000 sf

Impact

75% Reduction in Parking Spaces

70% Learning Spaces with Connection to Outdoors

27 Distinct Indoor/Outdoor Collaboration Zones

Economically Disadvantaged Student Population

Recognition

Architecture Award AIA, 2023
Education Facility Award AIA/CAE, 2022
Honor Award AIA California/CASH, 2017

TIDE

Spectrum IV

A lab building grounded in nature.

A lab dedicated to cystic fibrosis research embodies the serpentine path of scientific discovery, creating experiences that put scientists in touch with the natural world that inspires them.

Alexandria Real Estate Equities | San Diego, CA

VX-770
OH
H
NH2
-H2O

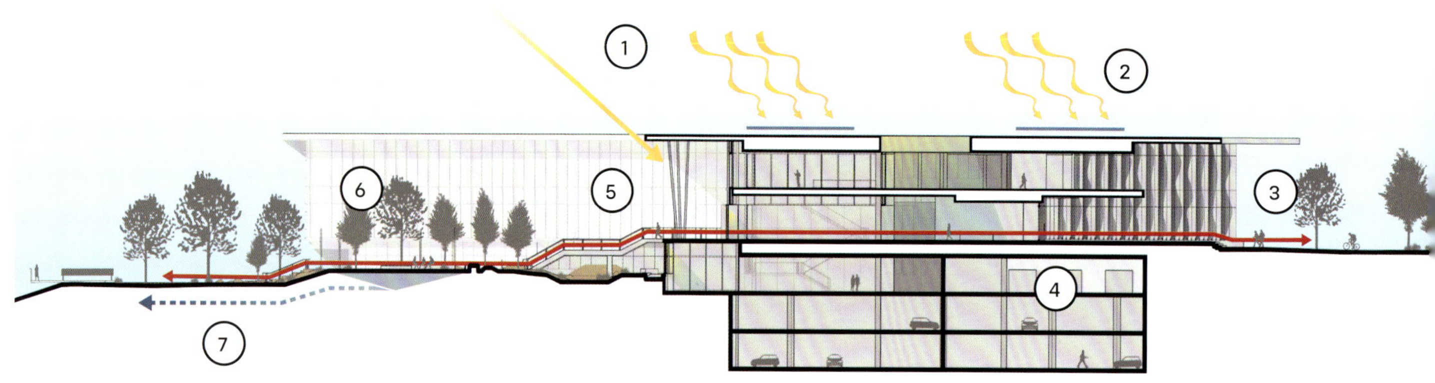
1
2
6
5
3
4
7

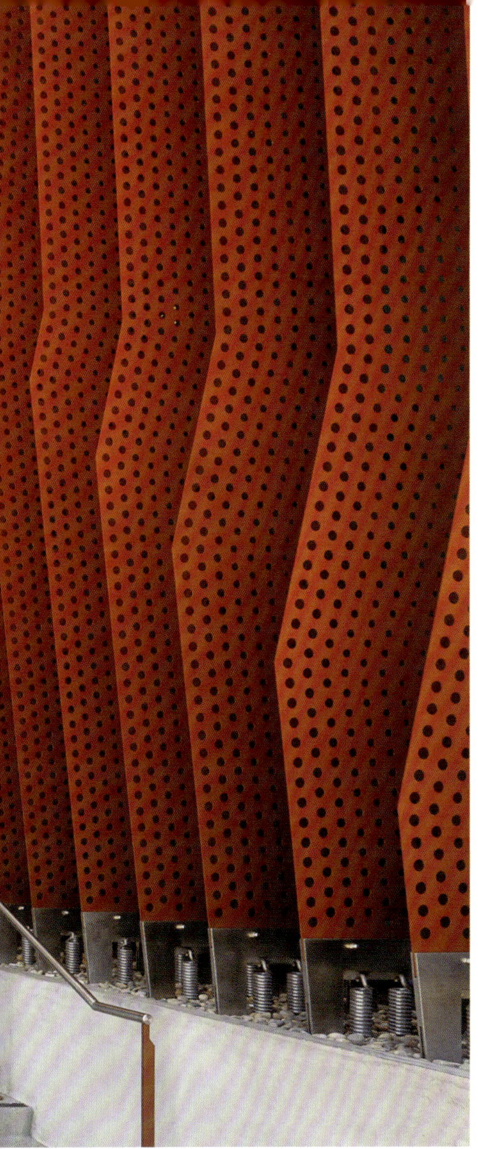

CONTEXT

Early in the design process for this San Diego lab building, a member of the client team described his guiding passion for science: "There is a constant thought. You may stray from it, but you always come back to it. It grounds you and gives you focus. It remains with you through the process and beyond." This interpretation of the scientific journey served as the inspiration and litmus test for all design decisions during the creation of a state-of-the-art new lab for developing cystic fibrosis treatments. Deeply sensitive to the building's location on the edge of a canyon in the Torrey Pines research cluster, the building and site put scientists in proximity with the site's natural beauty.

"This building inspires our scientists to do their best work. It was designed with the concept of discovery in mind from the beginning."

Paul Negulescu, Senior Vice President of Research, Vertex Pharmaceuticals

1. Natural Daylight
2. Photovoltaic Array
3. Performative Screen
4. Integrated Mechanical System
5. Outdoor Circulation & Active Design
6. Outdoor Collaboration
7. Rainwater Collection

OUTCOME

The experience of discovery starts on arrival, where a feature wall of sixty-two custom perforated fins lines the entry portal and outdoor amenity entrance. Their pattern and rhythm mimic the folds of the lungs, detailed with springs that enable them to move subtly in the wind. The fins bisect the two wings of the building, reminiscent of the trachea and lobes of the lungs. A daylit lobby provides a through-connection to a one-acre landscape of conference and gathering spaces. Walking paths wind through a native, drought-tolerant landscape with bioswales, basins, and wildlife habitats, terminating in a view deck with breathtaking canyon vistas. It's the perfect place to think and develop scientific discoveries.

INTEGRATION

From the start, designers, structural engineers, and landscape architects wrestled with how to fit the facility on the steep site, while preserving the canyon and meeting local codes. Early on, the team met weekly with the developer and the future tenant, exploring concepts and different placements. Multiple building forms were studied before engineers landed on two steel-framed rectangular wings connected by a central lobby. The V shape enables 100% of the occupied interior space to be filled with natural light and provides expansive mountain views throughout the building. By orienting the wings at forty-five degrees from the central core, structural engineers reduced the amount of structural steel needed to withstand the region's powerful seismic forces. The structure was buried five feet into the slope to respect and preserve the unique character of the California coastline. To protect interior spaces from the sun, designers and engineers developed a canopy that seamlessly cantilevers along the perimeter of the roof, extending out twenty-five feet in some areas. They also collaborated closely on the placement of the bouquets of thin tube steel columns that support the canopy, which shades social and collaborative spaces.

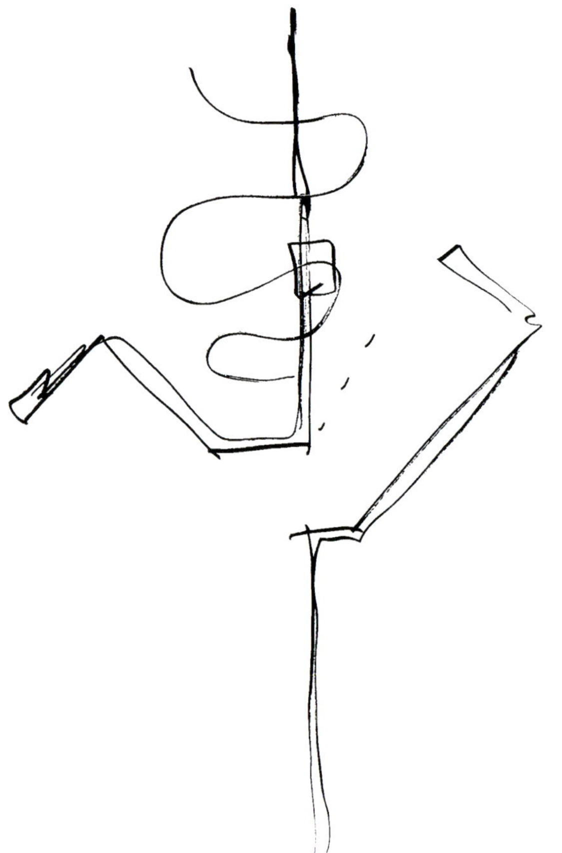

STRUCTURAL ENGINEERING

SKETCHING, MODELING, AND TESTING LED TO A V-SHAPED DESIGN, WHICH FIT THE FACILITY ON THE STEEP SITE, SAVED STEEL, AND LEFT AN ACRE OPEN FOR OUTDOOR ENVIRONMENTS.

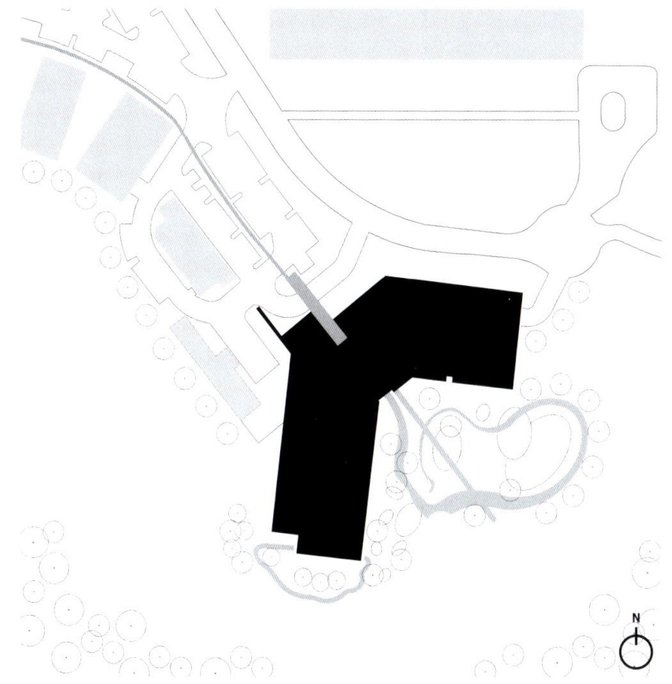

Performance

46%

OPERATIONAL CARBON EMISSIONS AVOIDED
(mT/year)

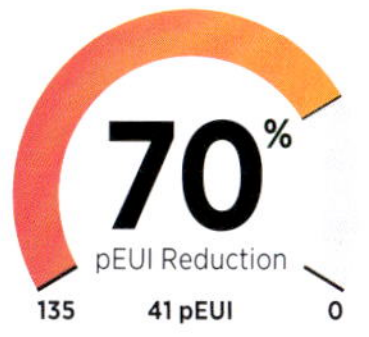

PREDICTED ENERGY USE INTENSITY
(kBtu/sf/year)

Met the AIA Commitment
70% THRESHOLD
at the time of design

Project	Workplace | Pharmaceutical | 2018
Budget	Confidential
Scale	Medium | 171,000 sf

Impact

100% of Lab and Office Spaces Have Daylight Autonomy

2.3K Square Feet of Program Converted to Exterior Meeting Space

70 Metric Tons of Avoided Emissions from Embodied Carbon Reductions

Recognition

Merit Award AIA San Diego, 2018

National Design Award of Merit IESNA, 2019

National Award AISC, 2019

LEED Gold

RiverRock Real Estate Group Headquarters

A new workplace helps people learn to work together again.

In the wake of the COVID-19 pandemic, nobody was sure if the traditional office was still relevant. A new net-zero-energy headquarters gave one company's "rock stars" a reason to go back to the office.

RiverRock Real Estate Group | Irvine, CA

"Every day, I walk in here, and I'm just so excited that this is our space. It reinforces our culture and our people and who we are."

John Combs, RiverRock Founder and Principal

CONTEXT

The big question: Why should people go back to the office? As COVID surged and ebbed, designers worked with the commercial real estate firm's staff to explore their culture, work habits, and long-term goals. The company calls employees "rock stars" and wanted its new headquarters to protect the staff's well-being. The freestanding, single-story concrete building chosen for the company's headquarters—purchased pre-pandemic—was unremarkable, a dark, closed-off relic of the 1980s. It had been largely untouched for thirty years. But it had good bones, including skylights that brought natural light into the interior space, and it was next to one of the area's busiest freeways, making it among the most visible buildings in Southern California.

OUTCOME

The renovated building is a study in hybrid workplace design, created at a time when the "hybrid workplace" was still being defined. A mix of private, semiprivate, and open zones caters to a diverse workforce, allowing employees to choose how and where they work. Ceilings were exposed to create large-volume spaces, while barriers to the outdoors were stripped away, flooding spaces with natural light. Wherever possible, the building's existing elements were reused, reflecting the staff's values. Flexible, leasable space created by the renovation has brought in new tenants, creating a lively village atmosphere. The rock stars rave about their new home. On most days, the workstations are full; a fun, collaborative environment offers them something they can't get from remote work.

INTEGRATION

Ultimately, the project was a tenant improvement, on a budget. Interior designers, researchers, and lighting designers worked together to choreograph the experience in each environment. Lighting, materiality, and furniture were designed around a shared narrative, with each zone reflecting established social and work goals. Lighting aids wayfinding and highlights the art, drawing people through the spaces and creating a rhythm and sequence to the different zones. Four small skylights were renovated to strategically infuse areas with natural light. From the main boardroom to the open office to the lobby, each space is highlighted, altered, and customized by the lighting. The result is a homey atmosphere, where individuals can control their environment and choose their own work style.

The collaboration between interior and lighting designers extended to the exterior, which offered limited options for energizing the forty-year-old building. At night, it is the lighting that announces the building to the world, with backlit fins establishing a dramatic new presence for the freeway audience.

LIGHTING

THE LIGHTING DESIGN HELPS CHOREOGRAPH THE SPACES, CREATING A RHYTHM AND FLOW THAT LEADS PEOPLE THROUGH THE DIFFERENT ENVIRONMENTS.

INTERIOR DESIGN

THE 1980S SPACE WAS REORGANIZED INTO ZONED ENVIRONMENTS HIGHLIGHTED BY NATURAL LIGHT, WITH FLEXIBLE SPACES THAT COULD BE SUBLEASED.

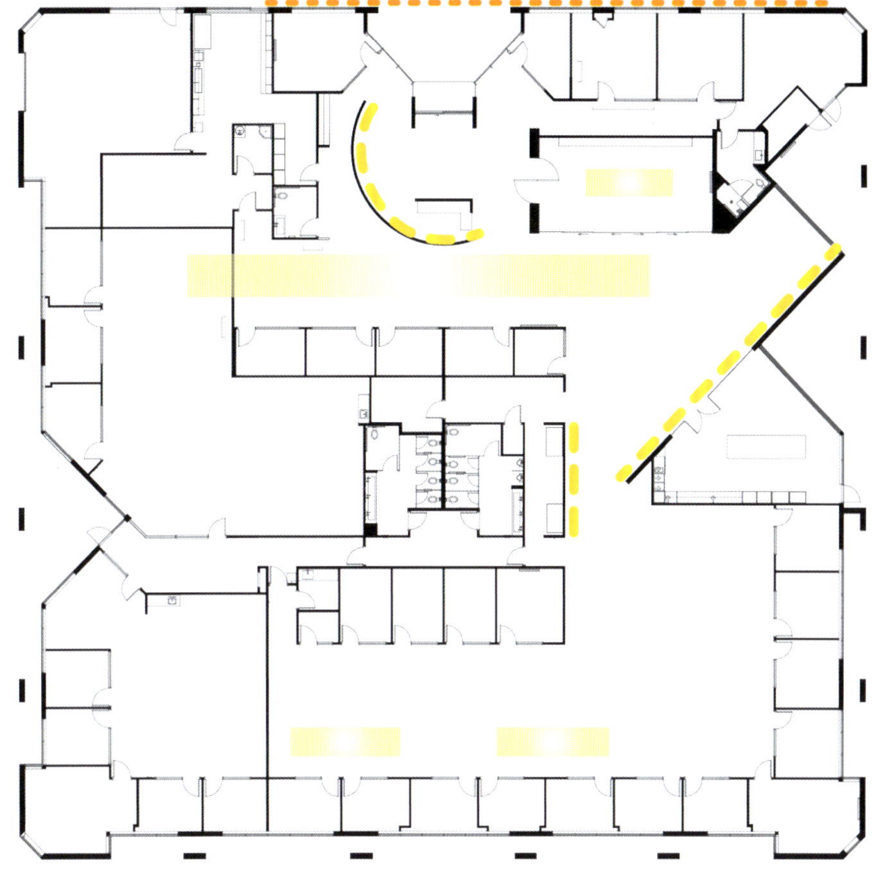

FRAMEWORK FOR DESIGN EXCELLENCE

DESIGN FOR RESOURCES

Reuse of the core and shell, mechanical systems, furniture, finishes, and art cut new material needs by 80%. Structural materials removed were crushed and repurposed as permeable landscaping.

DESIGN FOR ECONOMY

A cost-value matrix helped designers prioritize meaningful improvements in openness and flexibility, while cutting costs through extensive material reuse.

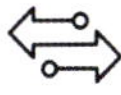

DESIGN FOR CHANGE

Pandemic pressures inspired a design for "whatever comes next," with flexible sublease spaces that can be easily absorbed by RiverRock or expanded to meet tenant needs.

DESIGN FOR ENERGY

Ample daylight, lighting controls, and a 138kW rooftop solar array achieved a net-zero-energy building without expensive MEP upgrades.

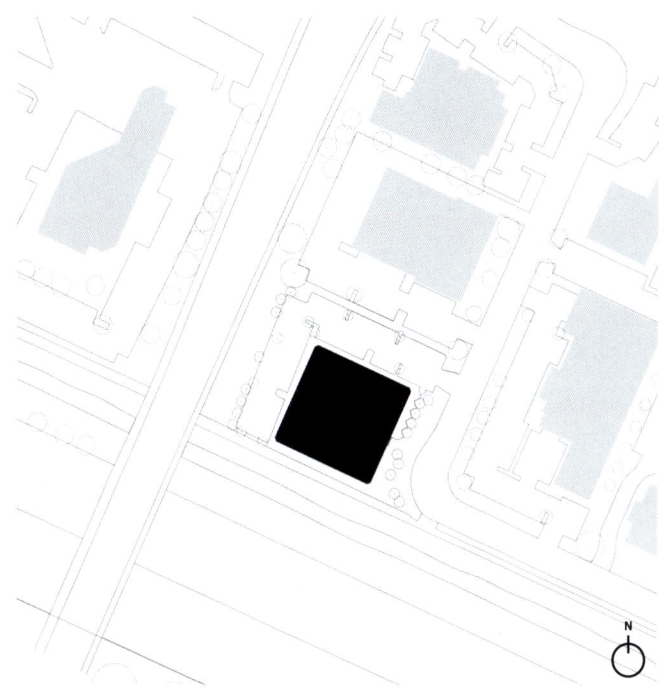

Performance

89%

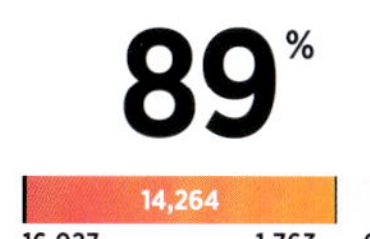

EMBODIED CARBON EMISSIONS AVOIDED (mT)

100%

OPERATIONAL CARBON EMISSIONS AVOIDED (mT/year)

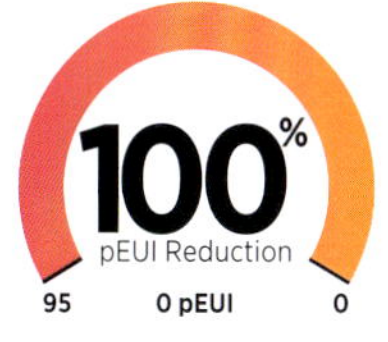

PREDICTED ENERGY USE INTENSITY (kBtu/sf/year)

Met the AIA Commitment 80% THRESHOLD at the time of design

Project	Workplace | 2021
Budget	$3.1 M
Scale	Small | 22,000 sf

Impact

80% of the Existing Structure Was Reused

138kW Rooftop Photovoltaic Array

80% Reduction in the Use of Finish Materials by Exposing Existing Surfaces

Recognition

COTE Award AIA Orange County, 2023
Citation Award AIA Orange County, 2023
Office Project of the Year NAIOP OC, 2022

Palomar College Learning Resource Center

A scenic library gives commuters a study destination.

Providing a compelling reason to stay on campus, the view from the reading room atop Palomar College's Learning Resource Center is the result of ten years of orchestration across four major, from-the-ground-up campus buildings.

Palomar Community College District | San Marcos, CA

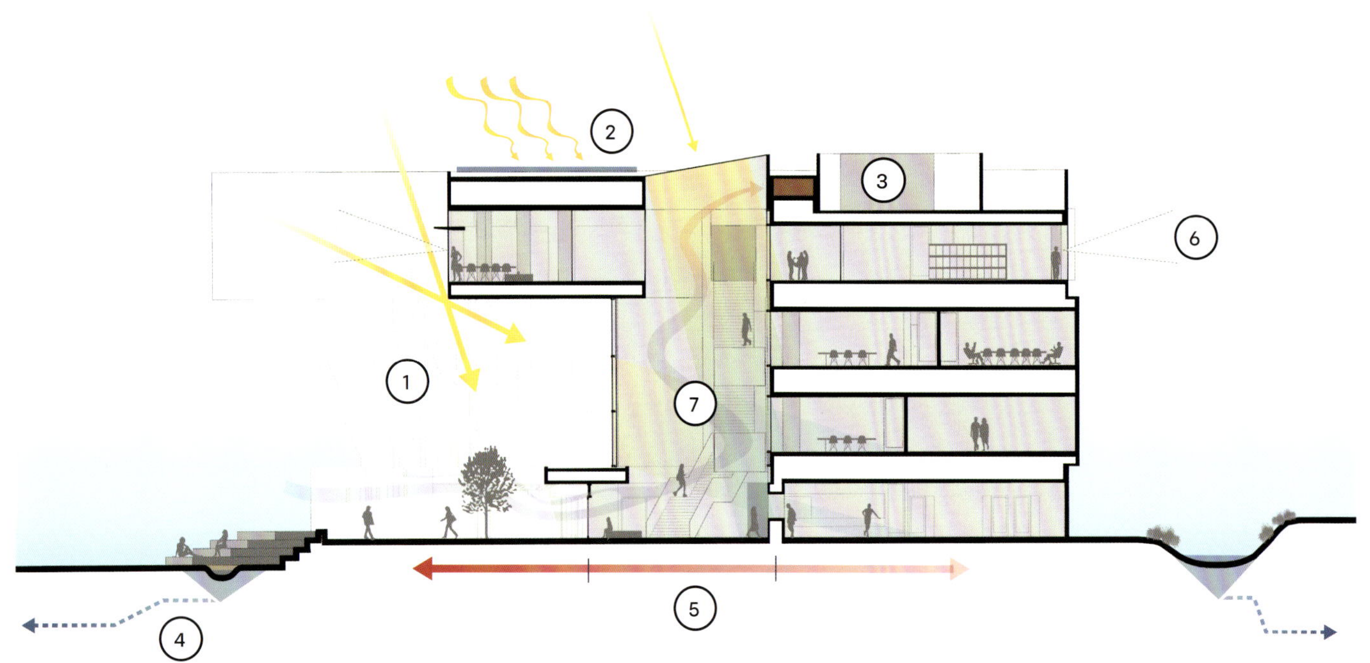

2
3
6
1
7
5
4

CONTEXT

Founded in 1946, Palomar College had grown by 2005 into a densely packed maze of single-story and portable buildings. There was no meaningful open space and no collegiate character. LPA developed a master plan for a transformation that would focus fewer, larger buildings around a central green. The Learning Resource Center (LRC) is the last piece implemented, offering a much-needed "home base" for students at the commuter school to study, get help, and build community. The design goals were to elevate the community college library with a bold expression and experience that would renew pride in the student population and community at large.

"We've already picked out our spots. There are so many places to sit and study, and I love the view. It's a really relaxing environment to do homework in."

■ Student, Palomar College Television, 2019

1. Self-Shading & Diffused Natural Daylight
2. Photovoltaic Array
3. Integrated Mechanical System
4. Rainwater Collection
5. Range of Acoustic Character
6. Views of the Valley
7. Mixed-Mode Ventilation

OUTCOME

The San Marcos Valley, known as "the Valley of Discovery" in Spanish conquistador times, continued its affiliation with discovery through the twentieth century as the home of the Palomar Observatory. Drawing on this history, designers imagined the LRC as its own kind of observatory, framing indelible views of the emerald-green canyons and Mount Whitney. Designers preserved that vision through the design and construction of the Multidisciplinary Classroom Building, Humanities Building, and Teaching & Learning Center, shaping building forms and rooftops to leave the views unobstructed. The LRC was designed around this moment, with the "floating" top floor extruded to make sure there is room for all.

INTEGRATION

The LRC's most dramatic features are the result of a decade-long collaboration between architects, structural engineers, and mechanical engineers on the Palomar campus. Of the three buildings that make up the core of the reimagined campus, the library was designed first, but built last. The clear views from the cantilevered top level of the new library and the public spaces between buildings were made possible by the holistic planning effort, which always anticipated the arrival of the library. In the humanities building, the major mechanical equipment was moved to the basement to keep the roofscape clear for PV and to optimize views from the future library. A new central energy plant was positioned in the back of the library to leave room for the plaza shared with the humanities building.

The library and its cantilevered top floor would not have been possible without detailed coordination between disciplines. The entire structural system was visualized and designed in 3D, allowing teams to explore different groupings and structural systems. The fourth level, the largest floor, was hung from the roof structure to protect the views and provide more activity spaces. Diagonal struts and strategically placed interior shear walls removed the need for large columns, creating shaded open space around the perimeter and a welcoming "front porch" for the facility. The found spaces were used to create flexible social environments and connect with walkways, helping to change the flow of campus life.

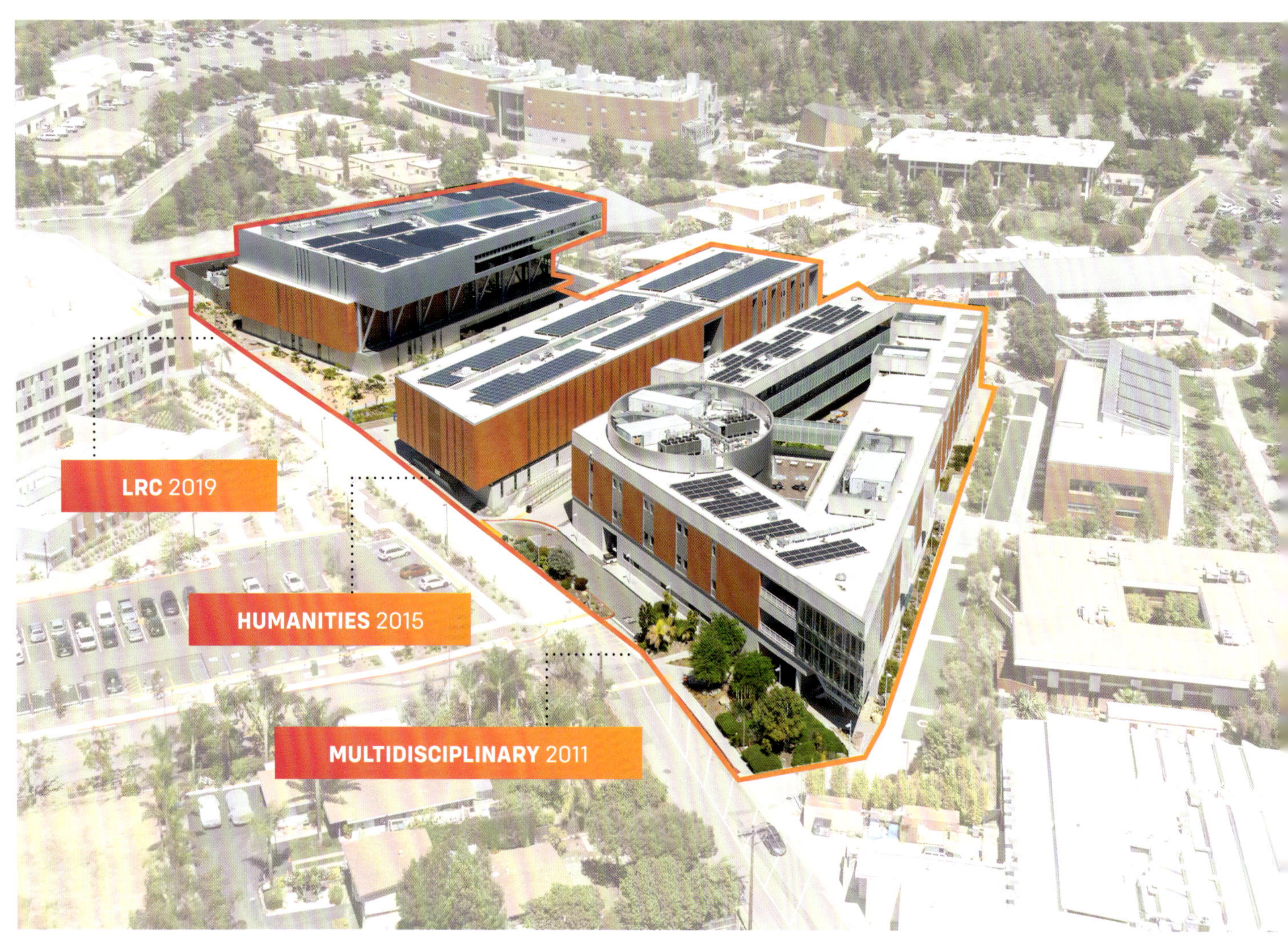

MECHANICAL ENGINEERING

FROM EARLY MASTER PLANNING STAGES, ENGINEERS WORKED WITH ARCHITECTS TO KEEP ROOFS CLEAR OF MECHANICAL SYSTEMS, FREEING SPACE FOR PV AND KEEPING VIEWS CLEAR FOR THE LIBRARY.

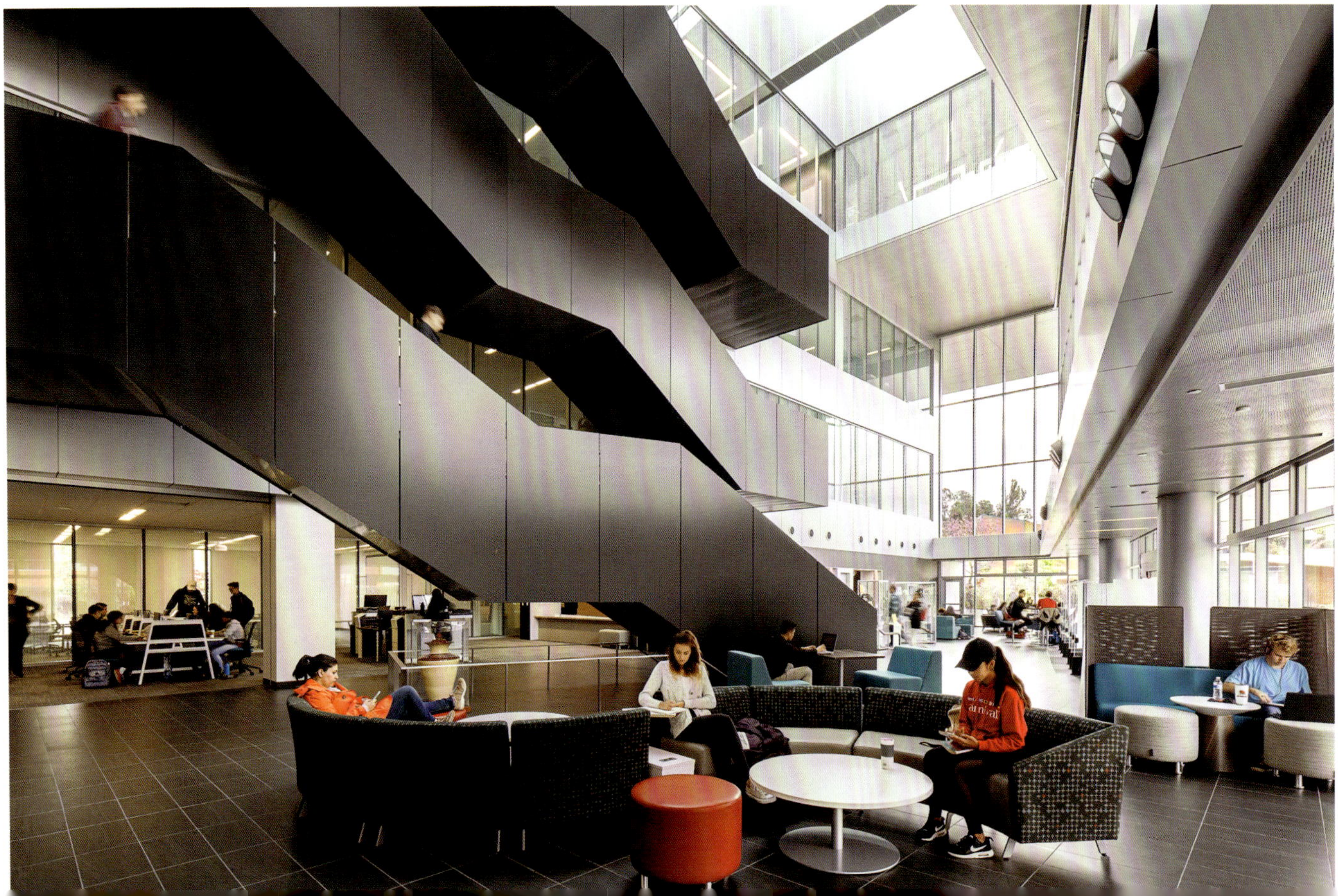

FRAMEWORK FOR DESIGN EXCELLENCE

DESIGN FOR INTEGRATION

Tapping into the valley's history of discovery, this modern observatory's design maximizes access to a view worth staying on campus for.

DESIGN FOR WATER

An amphitheater out front doubles as stormwater retention, using blue granite boulders excavated on site. 100% of water is treated on site.

DESIGN FOR ENERGY

Mixed-mode ventilation with operable windows leverages prevailing breezes, with an air-cooled, water-chilled central plant, 20% PV offset, and daylighting adding up to 30% better energy performance than Title 24.

DESIGN FOR WELL-BEING

Dramatic stair "rewards" physical activity with dynamic views at each landing. At the sky level, a panoramic view is provided to reduce cortisol levels.

DESIGN FOR CHANGE

Wide-open floor plates are a gift of the moment frame structure, which resists seismic forces without shear walls or braces that would limit future reconfiguration.

Performance

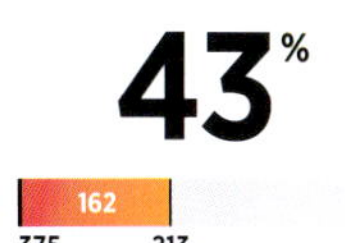

OPERATIONAL CARBON EMISSIONS AVOIDED
(mT/year)

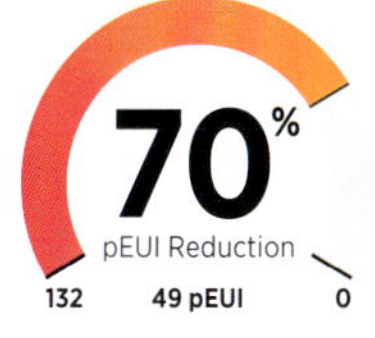

PREDICTED ENERGY USE INTENSITY
(kBtu/sf/year)

Met the AIA Commitment
70% THRESHOLD
at the time of design

Project	Higher Ed | Learning Resource Center | 2019
Budget	$47.5 M
Scale	Medium | 85,000 sf

Impact

75% of Occupied Spaces with Daylight Autonomy

20% of Energy Use Offset by Renewable Energy

Recognition

Award of Excellence SEAOSD, 2022
Award of Excellence CCFC, 2020
Merit Award AIA Orange County, 2019
Merit Award AIA San Diego, 2019
Honor Award ASLA, 2018
Award of Excellence ASLA, 2018
Award of Merit CCFC, 2015
LEED Gold

Tarbut V'Torah Campus Upper and Lower Campus Expansion

Opening up revives a struggling Jewish school.

When Tarbut V'Torah K-12 school decided on a radical new direction, their campus had to evolve from a cloister into a community.

Tarbut V'Torah Community Day School | Irvine, CA

CONTEXT

When the existing campus of Tarbut V'Torah was designed in 2000, it was in a climate of fear surrounding a vehicular attack on a local preschool the year before. The security of students was a top priority—but at the expense of their experience and engagement with the world. The resulting campus was walled off, full of opaque, disconnected buildings. In 2013, enrollment challenges prompted the school board to rethink everything. Initiated by a campus transformation, TVT traded strict religious alignment for a pluralistic embrace of diversity and shifted focus from traditional instruction to a collaborative, project-based STEAM curriculum.

"They rethought community and education to set the stage for their future. The result is a vibrant, inclusive and thriving school!"

AIA CAE Juror

OUTCOME

The design forges new connections to the community and within the campus. Three new structures break the program down, enabling every square inch of outdoor space to bring people together. Courtyards extend the indoor classrooms, and operable walls create fluidity between age groups and opportunities for mentorship. In contrast to the religiously freighted Jerusalem stone and sand-colored plaster of the existing buildings, glass surfaces create a window to the community, and reflective metal panels allow students to literally "see themselves" in their educational journey. The project successfully reversed TVT's student losses from 2009 to 2013, bringing the census up from 460 to 580 within three years of construction completion in 2017. Today, they have 800 students.

INTEGRATION

From the earliest goal-setting exercises, civil engineers and landscape architects aligned around TVT's mission to support "joyful learning." Stormwater management was elevated into an opportunity for hands-on lessons in sustainability and Jewish culture. Civil engineers helped develop a campus plan that turns the steep slope—a seemingly unusable space between the upper and lower school—into a valuable resource. The fitness building, tucked into the slope, unites the campus and forms the heart of a stormwater system dubbed "The Living Machine." On top of the facility, excavated soil was used to create a 4,000-square-foot green roof of drought-tolerant California poppies and succulents, which insulates the rooms below and provides a view for the classrooms above. Stormwater drains into a "discovery creek" paved with cobblestones and lined with plantings, where students can twist a faucet and play in the collected water. Interpretive signage explains how the water flows into an observation basin and is distributed into a biofiltration station, where it is naturally cleansed of pollutants by plant material and soil before recharging the aquifer. Nearby, in the shade of a pepper tree, designers created a genizah, an area for storing sacred artifacts, linking the past and present.

LANDSCAPE ARCHITECTURE AND CIVIL ENGINEERING

LANDSCAPE ARCHITECTS AND CIVIL ENGINEERS CREATED A STORMWATER TREATMENT SYSTEM DUBBED "THE LIVING MACHINE," WHICH IS EMBEDDED INTO THE CAMPUS DESIGN.

TIKKUN OLAM
REPAIR THE WORLD

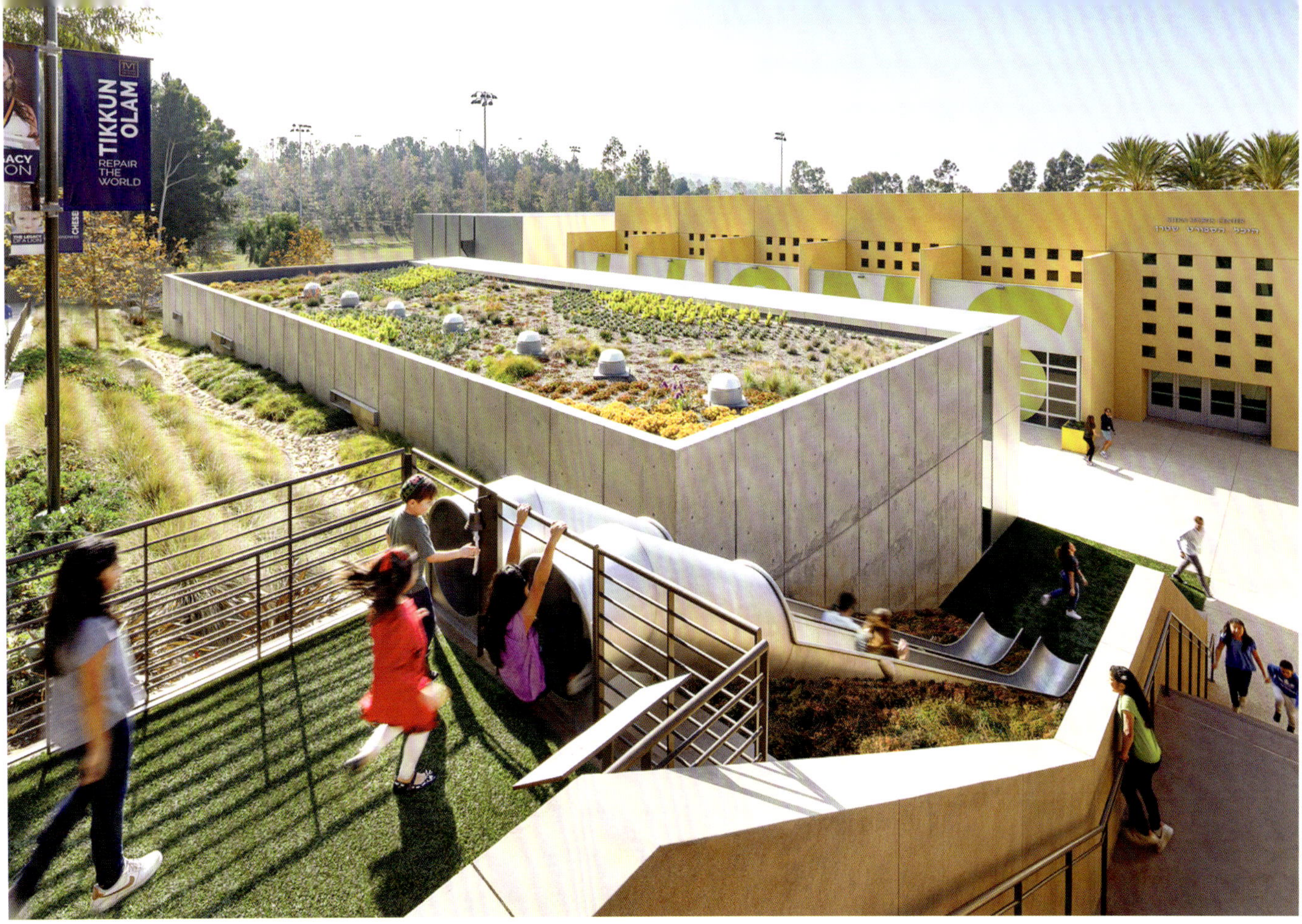

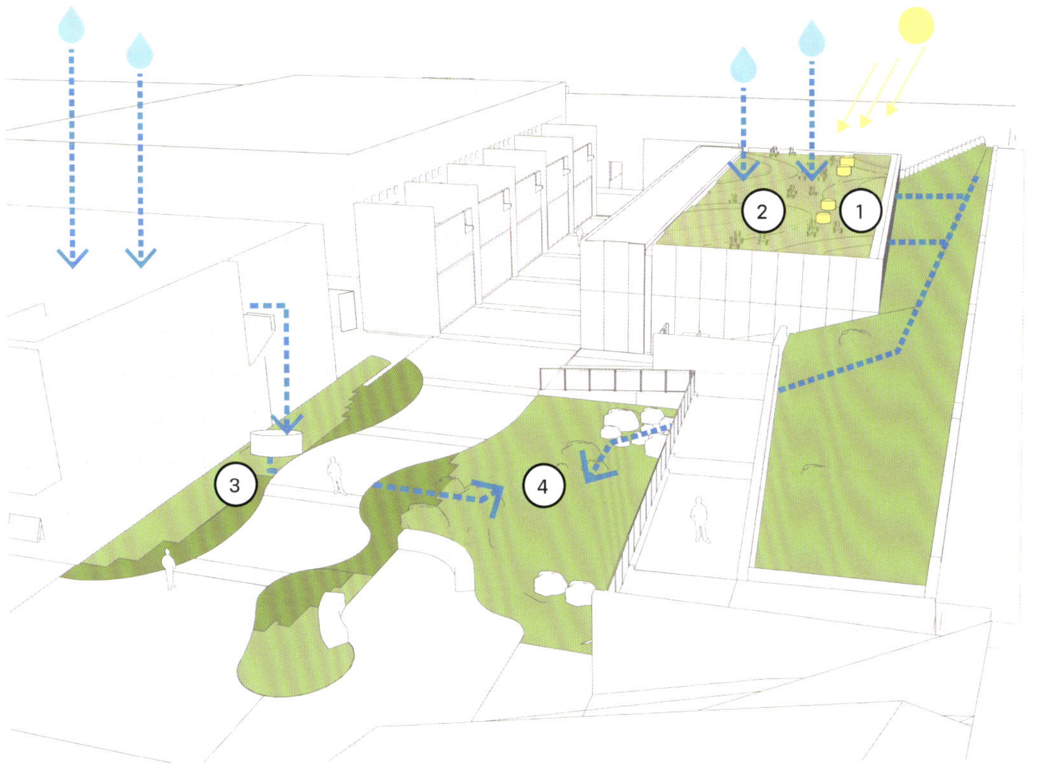

1 Daylight
2 Green Roof
3 Rain Well
4 Biofiltration

INCREASING ENROLLMENT

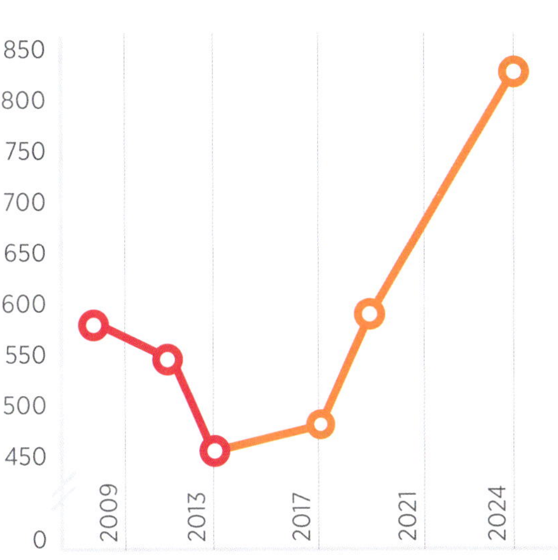

2013

AFTER THE LOSS OF 100+ STUDENTS, TVT DEVELOPS A BOLD STRATEGIC PLAN

2018

AFTER CONSTRUCTION IS COMPLETED, ENROLLMENT INCREASES BY 120 STUDENTS IN A THREE-YEAR PERIOD

2024

ENROLLMENT INCREASED 42% SINCE 2018

Performance

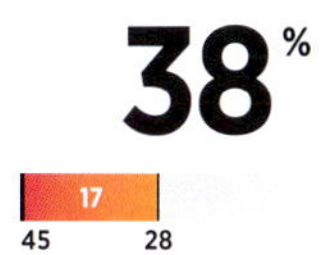

OPERATIONAL CARBON
EMISSIONS AVOIDED
(mT/year)

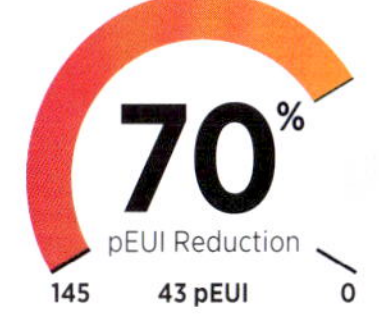

PREDICTED ENERGY
USE INTENSITY
(kBtu/sf/year)

Met the AIA Commitment
70% THRESHOLD
at the time of design

Project	K-12 | Private | 1997–2018
Budget	$62.7 M
Scale	Large | 30,000 sf

Impact

100% of Stormwater Captured and Treated on Site

100% of Occupied Spaces Are Naturally Daylit

100% of Spaces Use Mixed-Mode Ventilation

Recognition

25-Year Award AIA Orange County, 2021
Education Facility Design Award AIA/CAE, 2020
Citation Award AIA Orange County, 2019
Honor Award AIA Orange County, 2018
Honor Award ASLA, 2018
Award of Excellence ASLA, 2018

TRUTH
EMET
RESPECT
KINDNESS
REPAIR THE WORLD
JUSTICE
COMMUNITY
VALUES

Equitable Communities

Community perspective is essential. That's why we've developed engagement processes based in research—so we can meet the right challenges with the right solutions, making communities more resilient and sustainable.

PERFORMING ARTS CENTER

West Hollywood Aquatics & Recreation Center

A haven for community on a tight urban site.

In a community famous for its activism and engagement, an inclusive design process was critical to meet diverse needs on a tight urban site and give green space back to the neighborhood.

City of West Hollywood | West Hollywood, CA

OOD PARK

CONTEXT

West Hollywood is a dense, walkable city of 35,000 active and engaged residents. For the diverse community of seniors, families, celebrities, and LGBTQ activists, the old aquatics and recreation center (ARC) was a cherished cultural hub. Anchor to West Hollywood Park, it was the backdrop to frequent large-scale community events, including parties for *Vanity Fair* and the Elton John AIDS Foundation. In replacing the ARC, the city sought to provide more functionality on a smaller footprint, consolidating multiple buildings into one and expanding and revitalizing the park. A fifteen-month community engagement process brought together twenty-six stakeholder groups that included a senior yoga club, dog owners, and a local swim team that attended a city council meeting in Speedos.

OUTCOME

The new ARC creates a cohesive and interconnected community hub, meeting diverse needs while still managing to return space to West Hollywood Park. The complex structure spans an existing roadway, adds stories to an existing building, suspends two rooftop pools above basketball courts, and opens into the park through a cantilevered communal stair. The input received from community groups directly affected the program, which added two dog parks, a daycare, a roof garden, and a yoga deck. In the first year of operation, the new ARC hosted Pride celebrations, day camps, artist receptions and competitions, and became a popular spot during heat waves for older residents seeking a break from un-air-conditioned apartments.

"There were many community meetings, and the LPA team really listened to fulfill the vision of an exemplary aquatic center for the City of West Hollywood."

Cathy Blaivas, Former Historic Preservation Commissioner, City of West Hollywood, and Longtime Resident of the City of West Hollywood

FRAMEWORK FOR DESIGN EXCELLENCE

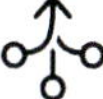

DESIGN FOR INTEGRATION

Replaces several buildings with a meticulously stacked program, giving footprint back to the city's only park and adding five levels of public, pedestrian-accessible rooftop.

DESIGN FOR EQUITABLE COMMUNITIES

Twelve months of community engagement brought together twenty-six stakeholder groups, spurring the addition of two dog parks, an AIDS memorial, and local public art.

DESIGN FOR ENERGY

To heat the pools, a variable refrigerant flow (VRF) system recovers thermal energy from the electrical and IT equipment. The energy-efficient building shell beats Title 24 by over 25%.

DESIGN FOR WELL-BEING

Light-filled, naturally ventilated spaces support well-being, while a surplus of flexible program spaces contribute to physical fitness.

DESIGN FOR DISCOVERY

Begun in 2014, the project pioneered research into responsible materials, contributing to the industry groundswell for open sourcing and influencing the Metropolis Climate Toolkit.

INTEGRATION

To maximize green space on the site, the facility needed to go vertical and make precise connections with existing structures on every level, including an existing second-floor parking garage and tennis courts on the roof level of another existing building. Moving the pools to the roof made the site plan work; however, this option placed the pools above the expanse of the basketball courts. In early sketches, it was clear there would be almost no room above the courts to handle the maze of structural, plumbing, and mechanical systems necessary to support the pools while aligning with the existing facilities.

Before the design phase officially started, engineers modeling options with designers made a critical breakthrough. By introducing a footpath into the design, they created a tall, narrow space between the pools, which allowed for the insertion of a thirteen-foot-tall "mega-truss" to support the pools' weight over the nearly hundred-foot span. Working side by side, structural, mechanical, and plumbing engineers were able to weave the pipes and ductwork through the trusses above the courts. Mechanical engineers found an extra few feet by locating a compact water-cooled variable refrigerant flow (VRF) system in a void between the recess of the pool and the roof deck. This helped keep mechanical equipment off the roof, freeing room for outdoor spaces to take center stage in a multistory environment that flows seamlessly into a revitalized West Hollywood Park.

MECHANICAL ENGINEERING

ENGINEERS WORKED WITH DESIGNERS TO FIT MECHANICAL SYSTEMS IN THE SPACE ABOVE THE GYM AND BELOW THE POOLS.

STRUCTURAL ENGINEERING

SPACE WAS FOUND FOR A THIRTEEN-FOOT "MEGA-TRUSS" TO SUPPORT MOST OF THE POOLS' WEIGHT.

"The new center is the heart of the city and is the direct result of years of collaboration between the community, the city, and designers. The ARC shows what can be accomplished on a tight urban site when people work together."

Steve Campbell, Director of Facilities and Recreation Services, City of West Hollywood

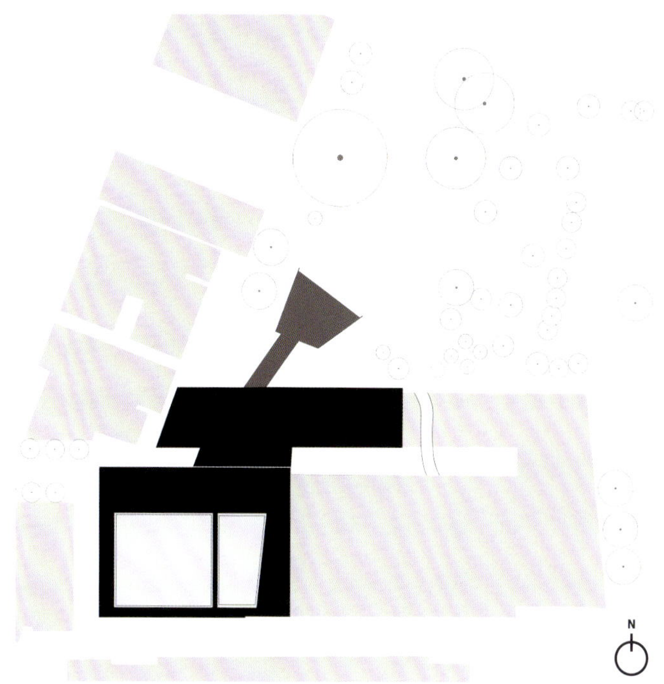

Performance

OPERATIONAL CARBON EMISSIONS AVOIDED
(mT/year)

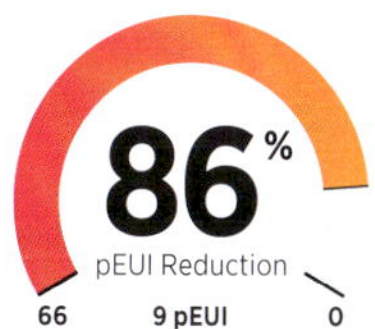

PREDICTED ENERGY USE INTENSITY
(kBtu/sf/year)

Met the AIA Commitment
70% THRESHOLD
at the time of design

Project	Civic | Parks/Recreation | 2022
Budget	$80 M
Scale	Large | 138,000 sf

Impact

26 Stakeholder Groups Engaged

72% Transportation Carbon Reduction from Baseline

94 Walk Score

62 Transit Score

76 Bike Score

Recognition

Structural Engineering Excellence NCSEA, 2024

Excellence in Outdoor Lighting SCIES, 2023

COTE Honor Award AIA Orange County, 2022

Honor Award AIA Orange County, 2022

LEED Gold

El Cerrito Multifamily Housing

Bringing high-performance housing to unsheltered San Diegans.

Large-scale, high-performance housing is an elusive target for designers and builders. El Cerrito, an eight-story, mixed-use supportive housing complex, innovates on schedule, construction method, and energy performance to make it possible.

Family Health Centers of San Diego | San Diego, CA

FRAMEWORK FOR DESIGN EXCELLENCE

DESIGN FOR INTEGRATION

The eight-story massing creates an urban edge, scaling down on the residential north side with four "fingers" of vertical housing.

DESIGN FOR EQUITABLE COMMUNITIES

The project creates a new model for both affordable and permanent supportive housing, supporting recovery for individuals experiencing chronic homelessness.

DESIGN FOR ENERGY

All-electric building uses passive ventilation, daylighting, solar heat gain control, centralized VRF, heat pumps, PV, and a solar thermal system to promote carbon neutrality.

DESIGN FOR WELL-BEING

Landscape embraces biophilia via vegetated roof terraces, vertical urban gardens, and orientation to channel prevailing NW breezes.

DESIGN FOR RESOURCES

The largest steel frame modular build on the West Coast uses recycled shipping containers adapted off-site to reduce cost and waste and accelerate completion.

CONTEXT

PATH (People Assisting the Homeless) has provided more than 1,500 units of permanent supportive housing using a Housing First model. Their largest project yet, an eight-story mixed-use supportive housing project in the El Cerrito neighborhood of San Diego, was their most ambitious. PATH sought to accelerate the construction schedule while targeting aggressive carbon neutrality goals. We explored a variety of construction strategies to meet PATH's goals before choosing off-site construction of 146 units of finished housing—a move that sped up construction and approvals by six months.

OUTCOME

The project tackles operational and embodied carbon while prioritizing rapid delivery—all key goals for PATH. Highly customized recycled shipping containers integrate natural ventilation, daylighting, and solar heat gain control to reduce operating costs. The biggest sustainability challenge of residential buildings—hot water—is solved with an electric heat pump boiler system with solar thermal, a highly efficient centralized VRF system, and PVs. Equity in the quality of spaces for residents was equally important. The building is strategically oriented and massed to create shade and channel ocean breezes, making the rooftop gardens, dog run, and social spaces pleasant year-round. The lushly landscaped outdoor spaces promote biophilia and encourage biodiversity while treating stormwater through biofiltration and using stored stormwater for irrigation.

"A shining example of the impact we can make on the world."

Elizabeth Carmichael, President, SDGBC Board of Directors

INTEGRATION

Speeding up the delivery of supportive housing "saves lives," says PATH CEO Jennifer Hart Dietz. The modular construction system provided El Cerrito with an opportunity to build faster, but working with shipping containers came with challenges. Early in construction, summer heat caused the steel modules to warp, slowing installation to a crawl. Designers, structural engineers, and contractors were able to identify the issue early in the process and work with the modular manufacturer to redesign the bracing system. Stabilizing the units accelerated the pace, allowing modules to be welded together seamlessly and stacked cleanly with minimal adjustments.

But that wasn't the only challenge. To get the project online as quickly as possible, modules had to be "plug and play." Architects and engineers met frequently with the modular builder to work through challenges, such as consolidating each unit's air, water, power, and data connections to make them easier to plug in and maintain. The teams were available to expedite the permitting process, often working with agencies that had little experience with modular residential. Ultimately, the modular approach allowed the healthcare clinics on the ground floor to open six months early, providing valuable services to a community in need.

STRUCTURAL ENGINEERING

ENGINEERS ON SITE WERE ABLE TO DEAL WITH ISSUES AND REDESIGN THE BRACING SYSTEM FOR THE MODULAR UNITS.

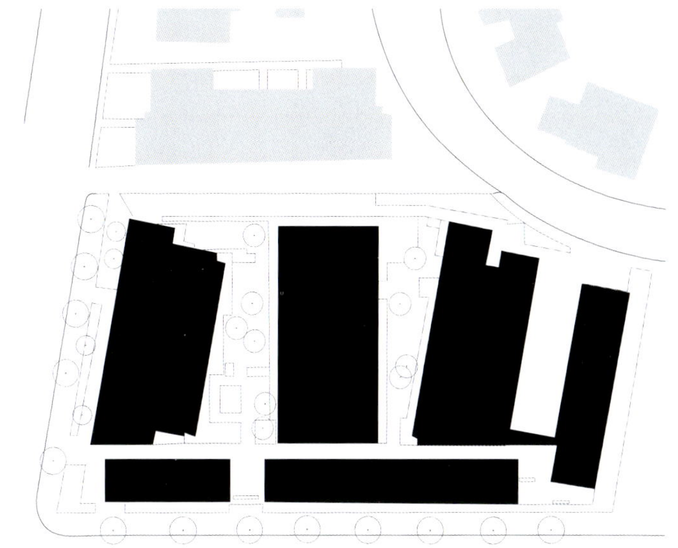

Performance

EMBODIED CARBON
EMISSIONS AVOIDED
(mT)

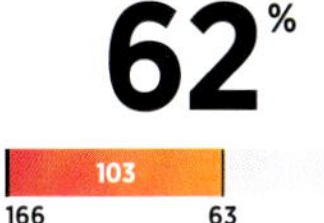

OPERATIONAL CARBON
EMISSIONS AVOIDED
(mT/year)

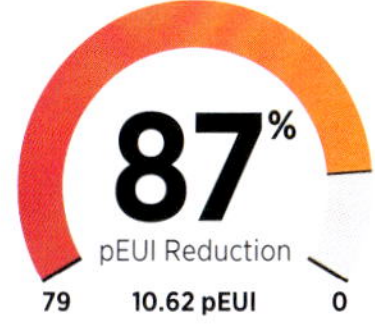

PREDICTED ENERGY
USE INTENSITY
(kBtu/sf/year)

Met the AIA Commitment
80% THRESHOLD
at the time of design

Project	Mixed Use | Housing | 2024
Budget	$43 M
Scale	Large | 225,000 sf

Impact

100% Electrified

45% of Energy Use Met by Renewables

Low-Income Community Population

Recognition

Sustainable Marvel Award
USGBC San Diego, 2024
Citation Award AIA Orange County, 2021

City of Eagle Pass International Bridge System Headquarters

On the U.S.-Mexico border, a new facility makes a city proud.

For the thousands of people who walk through the U.S.-Mexico border crossing at Eagle Pass every day, the city's first net-zero-energy civic facility is a welcoming presence.

City of Eagle Pass | Eagle Pass, TX

CONTEXT

Eagle Pass is a rural city of 28,000 people on one of the busiest border crossings in the U.S. The city's identity, culture, and economy are tied to the connection with Mexico; 95% of the largely lower-income community is of Hispanic or Latino descent. For people walking across the Rio Grande River on the pedestrian bridge, the city's facility is the first building they see entering the U.S. or the last building they see as they leave. In a city that often felt passed over, the new headquarters is a symbol of the modern Eagle Pass. The operations team had been working out of a "temporary" building for twenty-three years. The center seeks to elevate the experience for staff and the thousands of people crossing the border every day.

OUTCOME

On a difficult, sloping site, the design balances the functions and views with the reality of the blistering South Texas heat. An elevated, shaded pedestrian sidewalk softens the walk-up experience, creating a welcoming, relaxed environment for staff and travelers. Spaces are carved out of the building for different functions, from currency transfer to staff breaks. A covered deck with views of the river provides space for cross-cultural events, fulfilling a key priority for the city. Despite rising material costs, the design shaved $1.7 million from the budget, cut annual operational costs, and demonstrated that cities like Eagle Pass can have the same type of high-performance facilities as larger, wealthier cities.

"This building has really become an icon for our community that represents the connection between the United States and Mexico. It showcases what the City of Eagle Pass is about."

Homero Balderas, City of Eagle Pass City Manager

INTEGRATION

Net-zero energy wasn't part of the original plan. The city had never built a net-zero civic project. Amid the challenges of a border city, it was far from a priority. But in early meetings engineers illustrated how the building could approach energy independence by tuning the roof to leave room for photovoltaic panels and the use of an efficient variable refrigerant flow (VRF) HVAC system. One problem: The city had never bought or maintained a VRF system. To help staff feel more comfortable with the technology, designers tracked down two mechanical service companies in the area able to work on the systems.

But there was another problem: On the constrained, sloping site, where would they put the VRF system, while leaving the roof clear? By committing to the VRF system early in the process, the site planning, which included landscape architects, was able to carve out a tiny wedge of the site for the mechanical systems, which ultimately worked nicely with the planned orientation of the building. To further reduce the building's energy load, daylight modeling helped find the right mix of roof overhangs, window shading, and glazing percentages, without adding cost. The anticipated load informed the size of the roof, which was designed to leave space for PV. The result created an example to help the city address more energy-efficient buildings while remaining good stewards of taxpayer money.

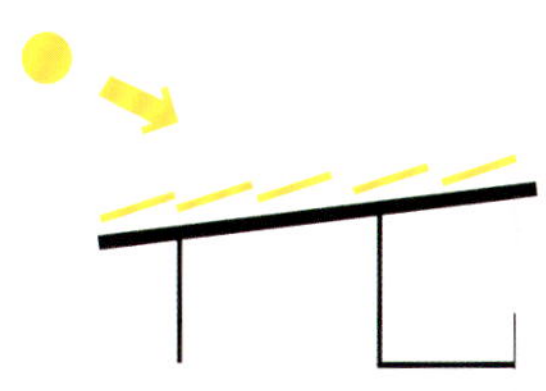

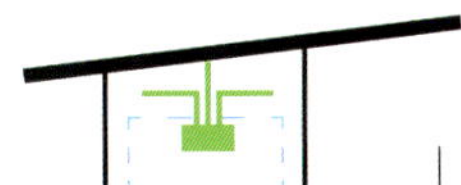

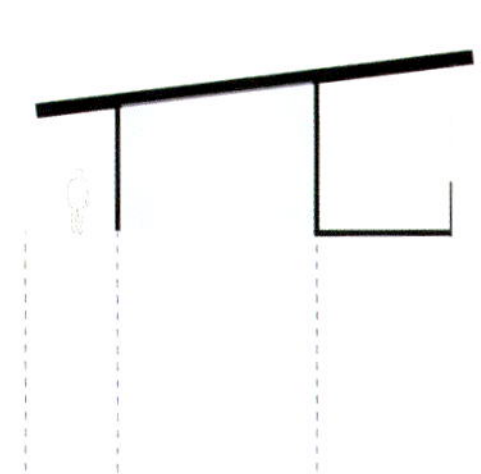

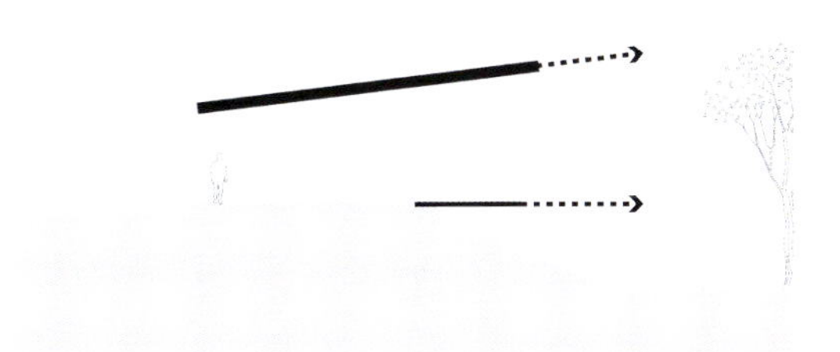

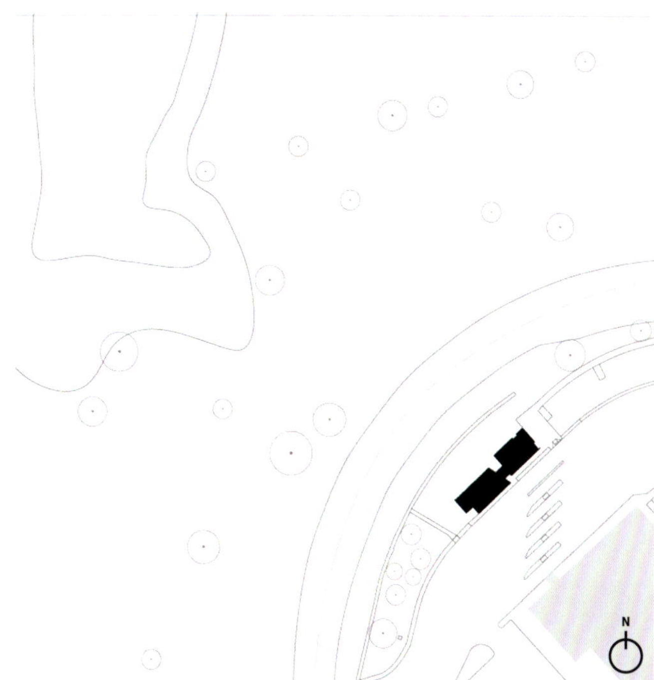

Performance

OPERATIONAL CARBON EMISSIONS AVOIDED
(mT/year)

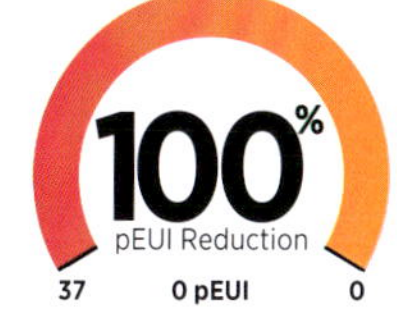

PREDICTED ENERGY USE INTENSITY
(kBtu/sf/year)

Met the AIA Commitment
80% THRESHOLD
at the time of design

Project	Civic & Cultural | 2023
Budget	$5.4 M
Scale	Small | 3,800 sf

Impact

50K	Pedestrians Pass Through This Port of Entry Each Month
$30B	in Trade Is Processed Each Year
23	Years Spent in a Temporary Facility

MECHANICAL ENGINEERING

THE BUILDING WAS ORIENTED TO MAXIMIZE SOLAR EXPOSURE FOR THE PV, MOVE THE MECHANICAL SYSTEMS OFF THE ROOF, AND HIGHLIGHT VIEWS.

CSU San Bernardino Student Union

Inclusion changes the narrative for underserved students.

Students at CSU San Bernardino felt written off despite significant contributions to the CSU system. Their voices were finally heard through the inclusive design process for a bold new student union.

CSU San Bernardino | San Bernardino, CA

CONTEXT

When designers first met with CSUSB students to discuss an expansion of the student union, they were surprised by a consistent emotional response. Students shared that they felt under-resourced in comparison to other campuses in the system. Despite academic achievements and the university's important role in the development of one of the fastest-growing regions in the state, the Inland Empire, students felt they weren't given the same resources as their counterparts in the CSU system. Restoring equity became a foundational goal for the design, which included engaging with more than six thousand students. Testifying to the effectiveness of the process, students voted to fund the project through increased tuition, even though many of them would graduate before they could enjoy it.

OUTCOME

The three-story building responds directly to the needs of students while making a bold statement on the fifty-eight-year-old campus. Uniquely diverse, with the state's largest proportion of Latin-American students, the student body includes more than a hundred affinity groups. These groups led the design of the top floor, a cantilevered volume that literally and figuratively lifts up minority students. The ground floor responds to a laundry list of student requests, including a bowling alley, restaurants, a bookstore, and pub. A repositioned entry opens to a new campus main street, the Coyote Walk, creating a vibrant center for student life.

FRAMEWORK FOR DESIGN EXCELLENCE

DESIGN FOR INTEGRATION

Expansion moves the "front door" to engage the campus's new main street. Building form leverages the "wind shadow" of an adjacent building, the self-shading of an overhang, and activated rooftop to expand the program outdoors.

DESIGN FOR EQUITABLE COMMUNITIES

Engagement with students shaped a project aimed at renewing pride and excitement in the underserved student community. Dozens of affinity clubs and minority centers create an empowering social hub.

DESIGN FOR ENERGY

Top floor is offset in two directions to shade the lower floors, with limited and carefully controlled west and south glazing exposure reducing pEUI by 78% and meeting the 2030 Commitment.

DESIGN FOR WELL-BEING

Orientation, massing, and localized sun controls bring filtered natural light deep into the building, while indoor-outdoor connectivity and mountain views introduce biophilia.

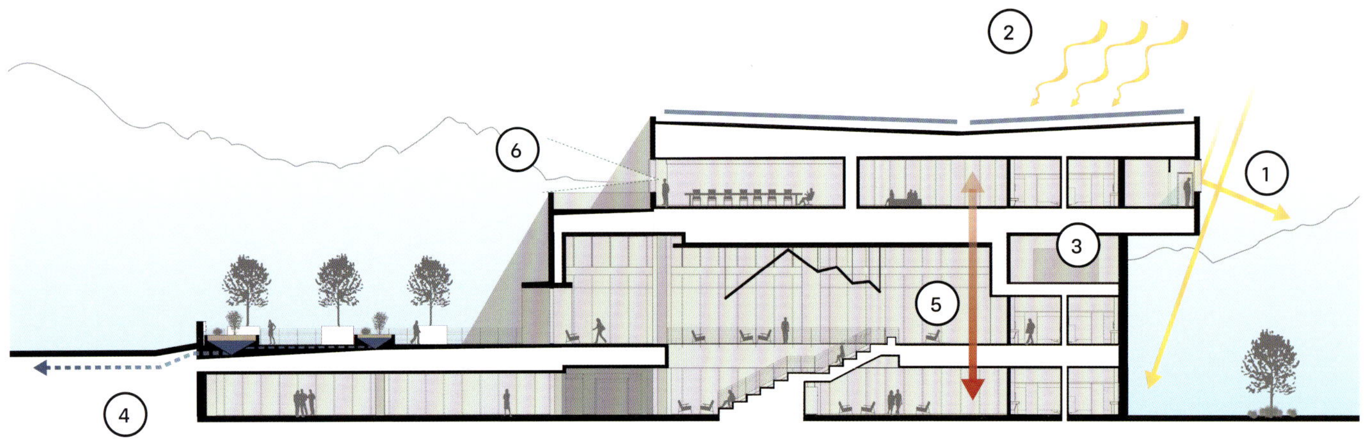

1. Sunshading and Diffused Natural Daylight
2. Photovoltaic Array
3. Integrated Mechanical System
4. Rainwater Collection
5. Range of Acoustic Character
6. Views of the Mountains

INTEGRATION

The expansion honors the students' desire to create a more equitable, sustainable campus with a focus on accessibility, connectivity, and environmental impact. Coordinating the new center with the existing infrastructure posed a complex challenge on the densely developed campus. Teams mapped out every roadway and every electrical, mechanical, and water connection to ensure every element fits together. With very little room to spare, and a mandate from the university to locate HVAC equipment indoors, mechanical engineers worked with designers to specify compact, efficient systems that would fit in interstitial space. This freed the roof for PV, further shrinking the project's carbon footprint.

Civil engineers used the site's fifteen-foot grade change as an opportunity to add vibrancy. The sunken main entry aligns with the campus promenade, sloping gently up through a landscape of protected social spaces to an elevated terrace at library level. All this added program space came at the cost of site permeability—a challenge to the team's early goal to leave stormwater unimpacted. Rather than a space-intensive bioretention basin, designers placed a system of retention chambers underground, burying them carefully to avoid disrupting plans for an expanded library.

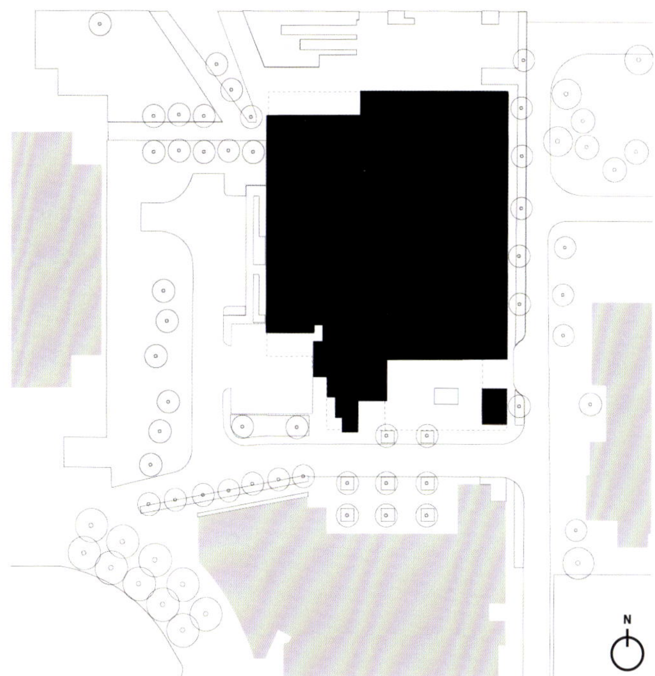

Performance

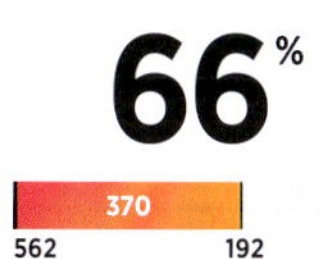

OPERATIONAL CARBON EMISSIONS AVOIDED
(mT/year)

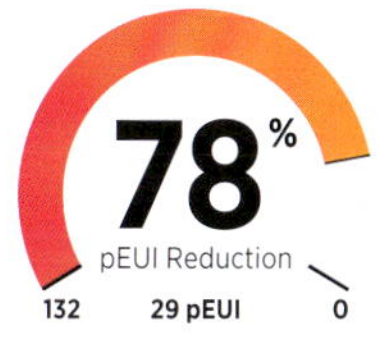

PREDICTED ENERGY USE INTENSITY
(kBtu/sf/year)

Met the AIA Commitment
70% THRESHOLD
at the time of design

Project	Higher Ed | Expansion | 2022
Budget	$68.6 M
Scale	Medium | 105,000 sf

Impact

30 Student Affinity Clubs with Dedicated Space on the Third Floor

70% of Students Are First-Generation Graduates

6K Students Engaged in Design Authorship

56% of Undergraduate Students Are Low-Income

Recognition

Merit Award AIA Orange County, 2023
LEED Gold

ENGINEERING

MECHANICAL AND CIVIL ENGINEERS WORKED WITH DESIGNERS TO FREE ROOF SPACE FOR PV, PRESERVE VIEWS, AND INTEGRATE THE RAINWATER COLLECTION SYSTEM INTO THE FACILITY.

Lanier High School Renovation

Culture and community light up a formerly windowless monolith.

At the birthplace of San Antonio's mural culture, a vital neighborhood institution with a legacy of inequality gets new life and new meaning, recontextualized to tell the community's story of resilience.

San Antonio Independent School District | San Antonio, TX

ONEY LANIER
GH SCHOOL
LDING 2

CONTEXT

Located in the urban core of San Antonio's Westside, Sidney Lanier High School has been an important center of LatinX culture since 1915. Its current academic building came about during an energy crisis when schools could be built without windows. Its community, 95% of whom face economic hardship, was excluded and overlooked for infrastructure and technology investment for decades, perpetuating educational inequality. Despite the challenges, Lanier's spirit shone through. Darkened classrooms became canvases for murals that adorned over sixty walls and became a source of pride and meaning. In meetings with stakeholders, designers learned of the murals' importance and promised to bring those stories of resilience to the forefront while transforming the building into a bright and healthy place of learning.

OUTCOME

The expansive brick building has been completely transformed. With the removal of its roof and top wall sections, clerestory windows now flood the interiors with light, while a central atrium serves as the community's new focal point. Dark hallways are gone, giving way to shared spaces with stadium seating and clear navigation. Formerly enclosed brick arches now house windows, illuminating the ground floor and connecting the facility to its surroundings. Honoring the school's mural culture, we worked with historians to preserve key artworks, establish a digital museum, and create space for future generations to contribute new murals and continue the story.

"It's like the *Wizard of Oz*—going from black-and-white to color."

Moises Ortiz, Principal, Lanier High School

INTEGRATION

Originally budgeted as an interiors-only project, Lanier High School's renovation had a budget limit of $200 per square foot. The team set a goal to introduce natural light and views to 100% of the formerly windowless building, but major surgery wasn't part of the budget. Architects and engineers developed a plan to remove the top eight feet of exterior brick and replace it with clerestory windows. Repurposed steel joists were used to reinforce new roof openings to lower costs and offer daylight in the middle of the building. Light wells on the roof were paired with new eighteen-by-eighteen-foot interior openings designed by the engineers to illuminate the first and second floors. Plans to use frosted skylights changed when a team member produced research supporting the importance of clear views in boosting mental health. That approach also led to the glazing on the ornamental brick arches, which brought light into administrative areas.

Yet, success still depended on the interior designers finding cost-effective ways to deliver the type of modern learning spaces that Lanier students had never experienced. Simple finishes were found for most spaces, which were designed around flexibility and efficiency. Funds were saved for the special moments that make the school unique, such as spotlighting the community's famed murals in the main hall. Together, the budget stretching preserved the legacy of a school laden with memories and meaning for the community, while creating a resilient, healthy facility for future generations.

EXISTING BUILDING MASSING

Minimal access to daylight.

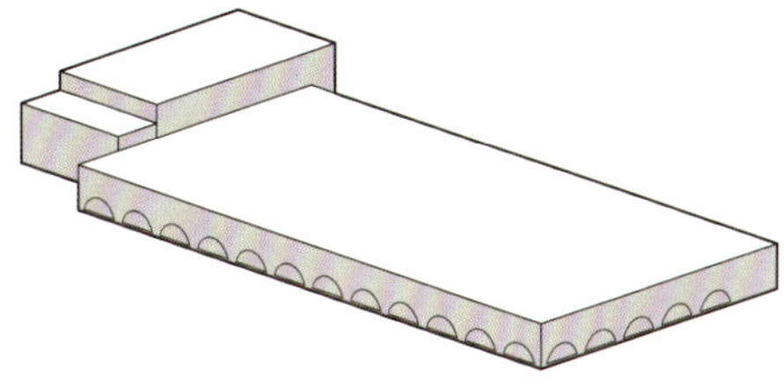

CUT OPENINGS IN THE ROOF AND THE SECOND FLOOR

Introduce more light to interior spaces.

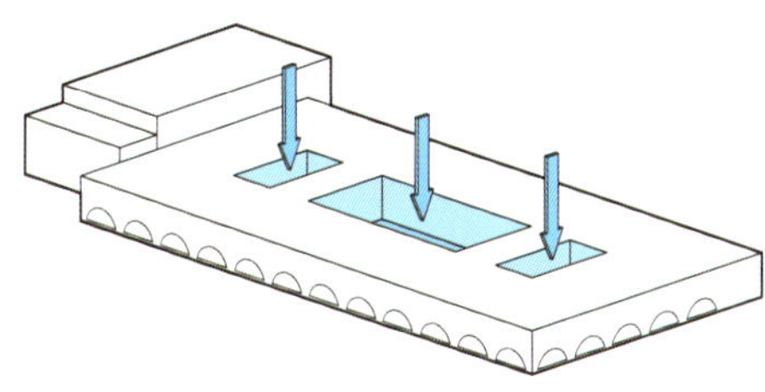

NOTCH FACADE FOR ENTRY

Carve out entrances to connect community and campus, infill arch windows to extend programs area, while bringing natural light to all interior classrooms.

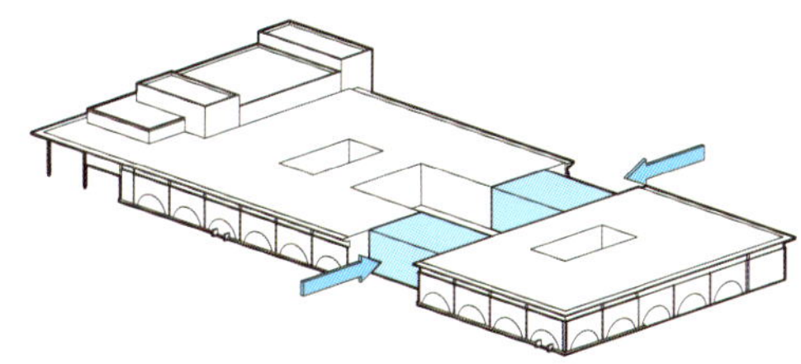

REMOVE TOP EIGHT FEET OF BRICK FOR CONTINUOUS CLERESTORY

With new skylights, exterior/interior clerestories, and arch windows, the building form maximizes daylight exposure while providing lighting to all interior spaces.

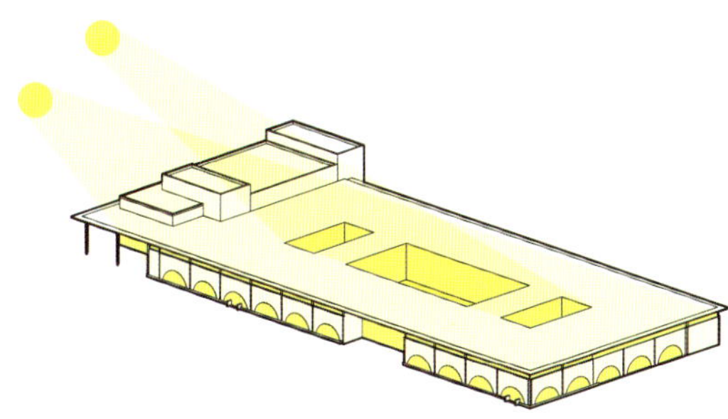

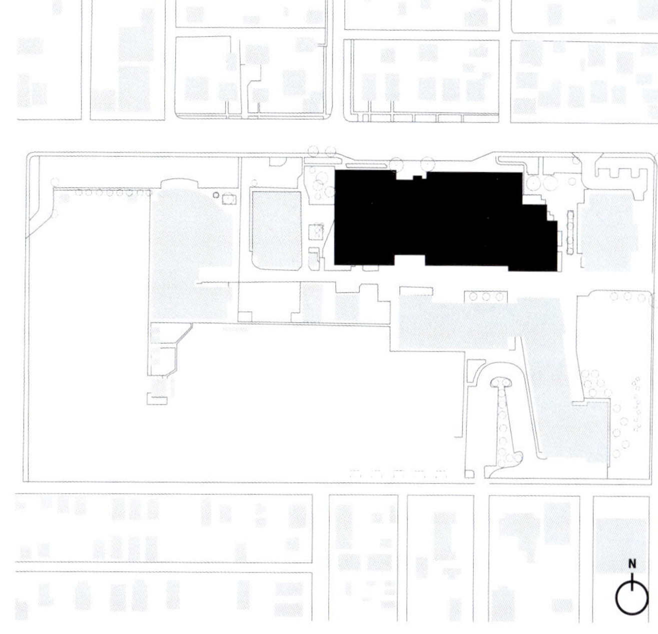

Performance

42%

EMBODIED CARBON EMISSIONS AVOIDED
(mT)

38%

261
684
423
0

OPERATIONAL CARBON EMISSIONS AVOIDED
(mT/year)

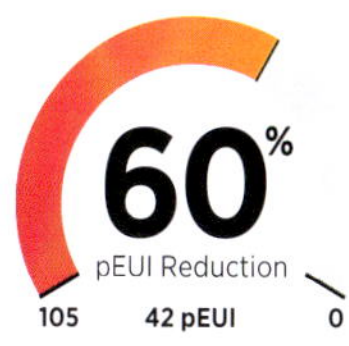

PREDICTED ENERGY USE INTENSITY
(kBtu/sf/year)

Project	K-12 | Renovation | 2022
Budget	$35.2 M
Scale	Medium | 172,725 sf

Impact

75% of Occupied Spaces with Daylight Autonomy

14.3K Square Feet of Glass Was Added to the Project

Economically Disadvantaged Student Population

Recognition

COTE Award AIA San Antonio, 2024
Education Facility Design Award AIA/CAE, 2024
Community Award AIA San Antonio, 2022

EXIT

VICA

Contextual Response

Climate change demands creativity and persistence in adapting to new conditions and improving our relationship with nature and the built environment. This looks different in every region and every climate zone.

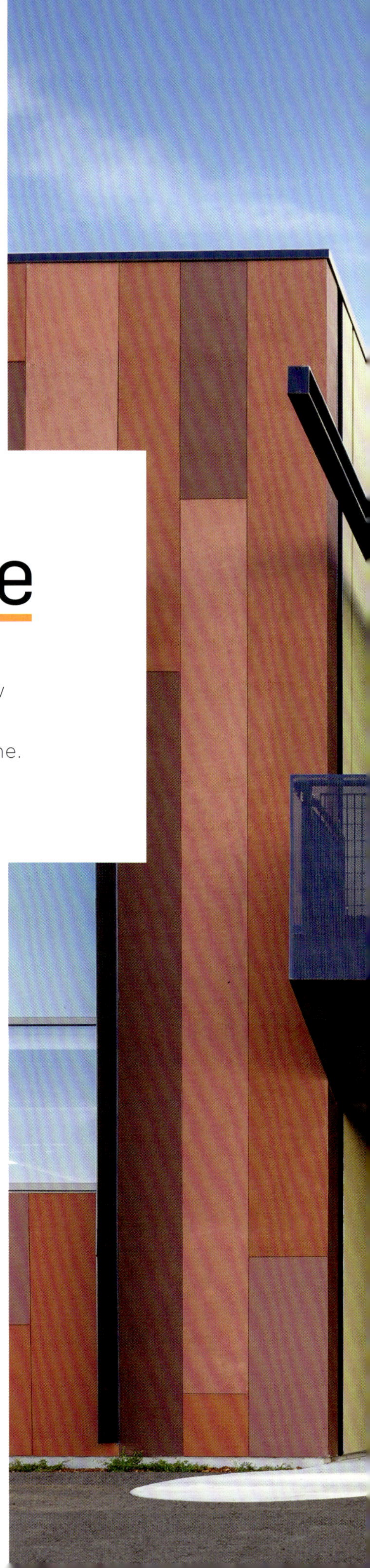

CSU San Bernardino Center for Global Innovation

A shield against "devil winds" expands student collaboration.

The scorching Santa Ana winds make CSU San Bernardino (CSUSB) an unforgiving place. Challenged to create a second home for an international student community far from their own, the integrated team had to tame the environment.

CSU San Bernardino | San Bernardino, CA

FRAMEWORK FOR DESIGN EXCELLENCE

DESIGN FOR INTEGRATION

Shifted and folded floor plates form a diverse array of indoor and outdoor social and learning spaces, with a central Global Gallery rising three stories to create a hub for international students.

DESIGN FOR WATER

Infiltration gardens surrounding the building filter 100% of site and roof water runoff and promote biodiversity.

DESIGN FOR ENERGY

LEED Platinum building uses displacement ventilation, operable windows, sunshades, and a 160kW array to perform 26% better than Title 24.

CONTEXT

CSUSB's large international student population needed a gathering place—a place for educational and cultural exchange that would foster community for a diverse population where 70% of graduates are the first in their families to receive a degree. Indoor/outdoor connectivity was critical to the designers' vision of a "global gallery" deeply connected to the life of the campus, and to the school's aggressive sustainability goals. The need to protect outdoor spaces from the blistering desert winds became a fundamental design challenge, shaping the entire building.

"We didn't have much usable outdoor space, and students really didn't congregate outside. But in just the short time the Center for Global Innovation has been open, it's become a heavily utilized site that offers students an amazing interaction space."

Jennifer Sorenson, Associate Vice President of Facilities Planning & Management, CSU San Bernardino

DESIGN FOR WELL-BEING

Provides much-needed access to outdoor space protected from the wind and sun, with light-filled indoor spaces and elevated view decks connecting students to nature.

OUTCOME

Architects and engineers worked closely to sculpt the building form with a series of shifts and folds in the floor plates, carving out two expansive outdoor spaces for learning and socializing. On the ground floor, a monumental overhang creates a towering outdoor volume safe from the predominant winds and sun. On the roof, a glass wind screen and light-filtering trellis protect an outdoor terrace and give students a scenic view of the San Bernardino Mountains. The roof supports a 160kW photovoltaic array, offsetting 50% of energy use and contributing to LEED Platinum certification.

INTEGRATION

Engineers were central in shaping a resilient, low-carbon building that balances seismic demands, desert conditions, and the need for inviting student spaces. The bold gesture at its center—a cantilevered third floor sheltering an open-air lounge along the Coyote Walk—required precise structural choreography. Buckling restrained braces provide resilience with minimal materials, while columns evoke a grove of trees. Their arrangement, informal but intentional, preserves gathering areas that a conventional grid would disrupt, while carefully avoiding the need for additional steel. Landscape architects worked with the engineers to develop the spaces in between the columns, creating links to the larger campus. Working beside structural engineers, the mechanical engineers used energy modeling—groundbreaking, at the time—to shape the facade and interior spaces. Glass, limited to 35% of the building skin rather than the standard 40%, is concentrated where overhangs and vertical fins mitigate solar heat. Natural ventilation, rare in desert buildings, doubles as a smoke-evacuation system while providing seasonal comfort and fresh air with minimal energy use. Early coordination with engineers found indoor space for mechanical equipment, protecting it from the harsh desert conditions, while meeting CSU's strict standards for floor plan efficiency. This left the rooftop free for solar panels, contributing to a near-net-zero design.

STRUCTURAL ENGINEERING

MODELING BASED ON DIFFERENT FACTORS HELPED DEVELOP A STACKED STRUCTURAL SYSTEM WITH THE DISTINCTIVE CANTILEVERED THIRD FLOOR, WHICH CREATED SHADED OUTDOOR SPACE FOR STUDENTS.

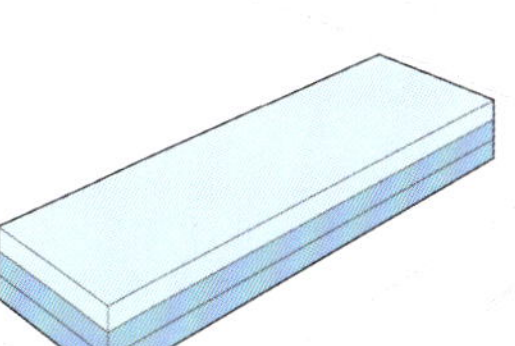

PROGRAM ARRANGEMENT

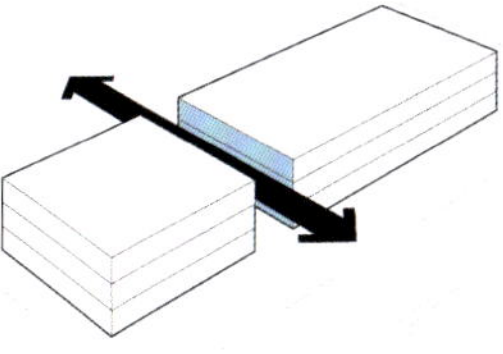

SITE CIRCULATION

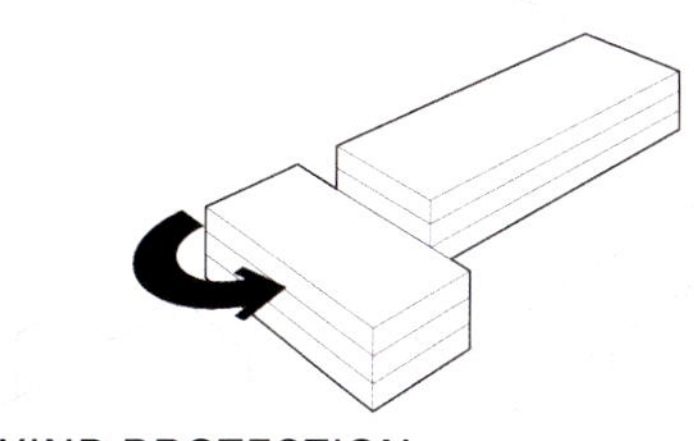

WIND PROTECTION

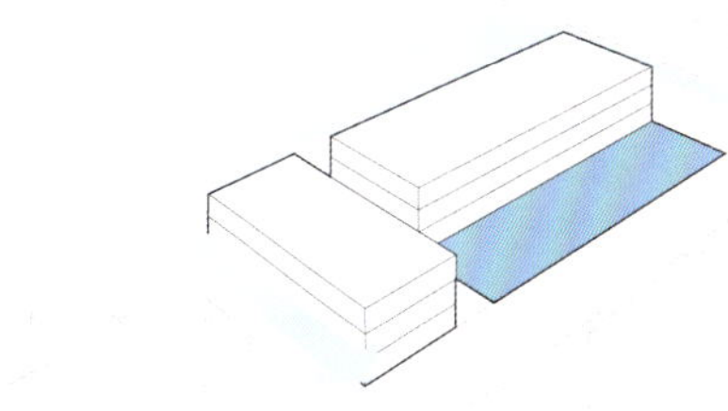

OUTDOOR LOUNGE

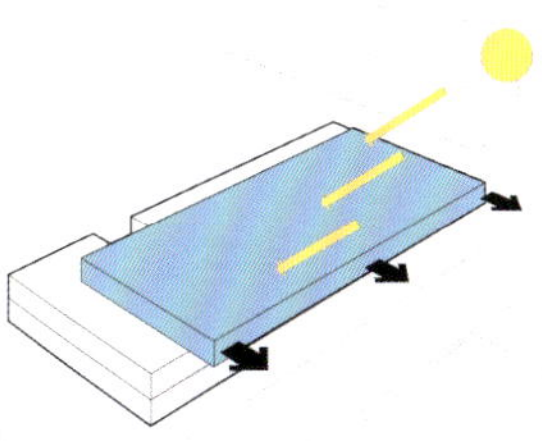

SUN SHELTER

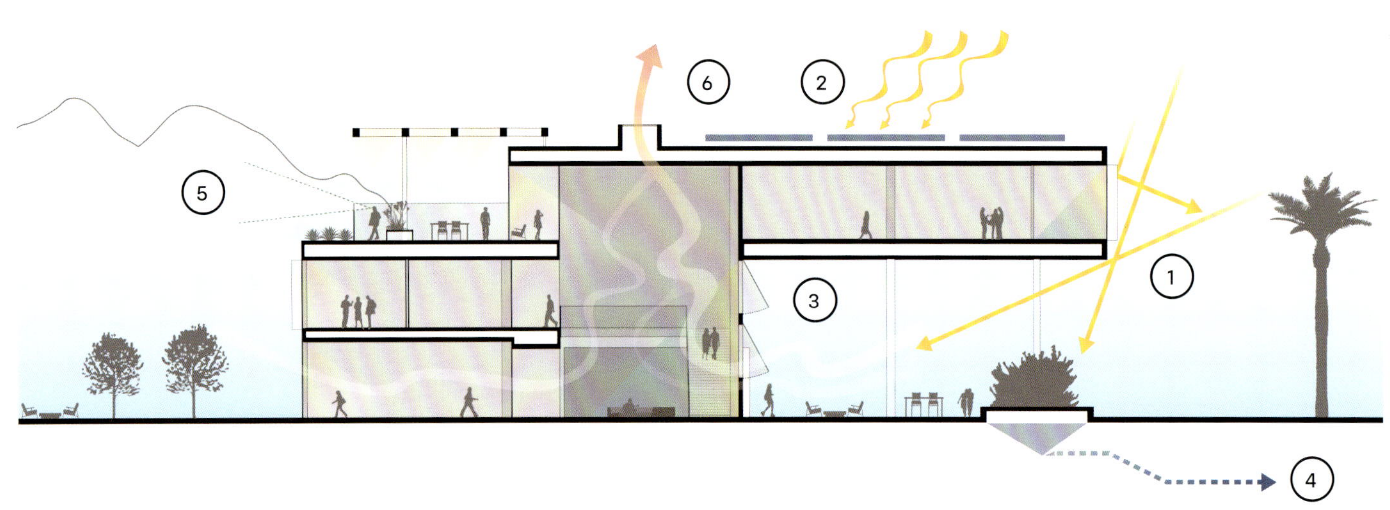
6
2
5
3
1
4

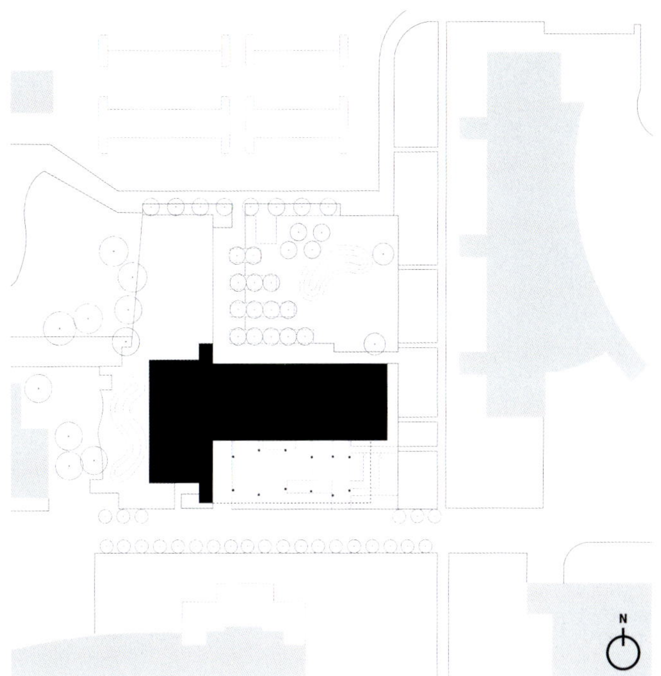

Performance

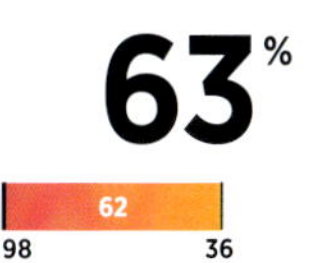

OPERATIONAL CARBON
EMISSIONS AVOIDED
(mT/year)

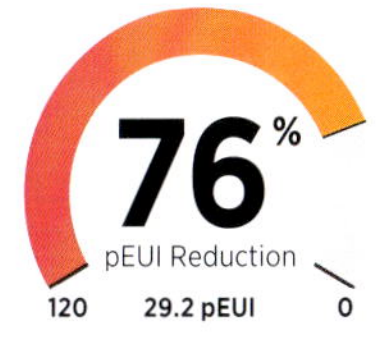

PREDICTED ENERGY
USE INTENSITY
(kBtu/sf/year)

Met the AIA Commitment
70% THRESHOLD
at the time of design

Project	Higher Ed | Renovation/Expansion | 2019
Budget	$41.5 M
Scale	Medium | 70,000 sf

1. Sunshading and Diffused Natural Daylight
2. Photovoltaic Array
3. Operable Windows and Natural Ventilation
4. Rainwater Collection
5. Views of the Mountains
6. Building Relief Fans

Impact

40mph Speed of Average Wind Gust on Campus

15K Square Feet of Protected Outdoor Program Space

100% Atrium Mixed-Mode Ventilation

Recognition

Municipal Green Building Award
USGBC, 2020

Honor Award AIA Inland Empire, 2020

Citation Award AIA Orange County, 2017

LEED Platinum

The
Globa

General Marshall Middle School

New urbanist ideals come to life on a middle school campus.

On an odd-shaped ten-acre site that was once the runway for Austin's municipal airport, a new three-story middle school lives up to the values of a thriving urbanist neighborhood.

Austin Independent School District | Austin, TX

"The design process was really collaborative, and I enjoyed that. We had community members, people who are now members of our board, teachers, and families who were able to input their ideas for what they wanted for their kids. And LPA was able to bring that to life."

Jordan Benson, Principal, General Marshall Middle School

CONTEXT

The Mueller District, a seven-hundred-acre redevelopment of Austin's old municipal airport, was designed as a transit-oriented, pedestrian-friendly model of urbanism and sustainability. It was the first neighborhood in Texas to earn LEED for Neighborhood Development (LEED ND) Stage 3 Gold Certification. The middle school was intended as a landmark at the end of a promenade, on the edge of a dense residential district. The site is less than a mile from a transit center, a key element of the district's multimodal, pedestrian-friendly master plan. Helping families stay out of their cars is one of the district's key priorities. District leaders had never built a school in this type of environment. They wanted a campus focused on interdisciplinary, project-driven learning that would "reinvent the urban school experience."

OUTCOME

The final design reflects the work of a sixteen-member stakeholder group that met regularly to explore neighborhood needs and the district's master plan. To accommodate the district's programming goals, the integrated design team went vertical. The three-story, 130,000-square-foot main campus is wrapped around a central courtyard, which is activated to support the academic, social, emotional, and active spirit of young learners. The campus links to the neighborhood and the local transit station with ten-foot-wide sidewalks, a network of tree-lined bike lanes, and walking trails. The building moved up to the property line, putting arts and STEM spaces on display. Throughout the campus, conservation strategies are highlighted, providing teaching tools that reflect the urbanist district's core values.

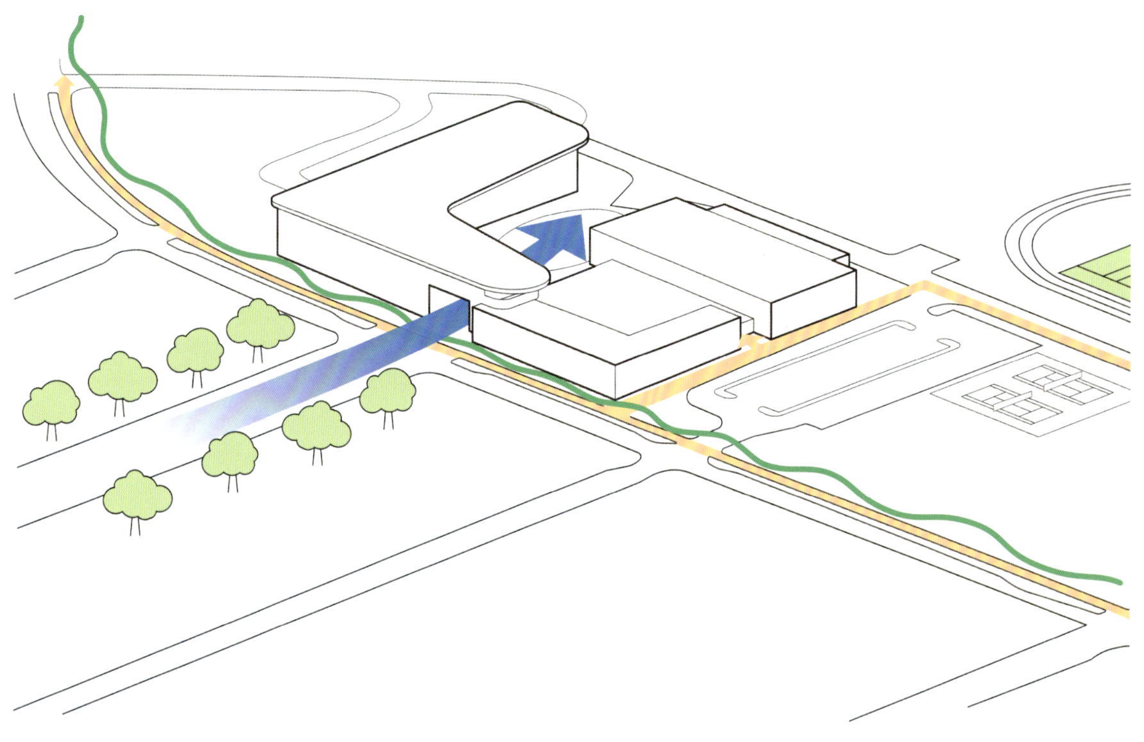

LANDSCAPE ARCHITECTURE

A MULTIDISCIPLINE TEAM ORIENTED THE CAMPUS TO CONNECT TO A NEIGHBORHOOD PROMENADE AND PROMOTE WALKING AND LINKS TO MASS TRANSIT.

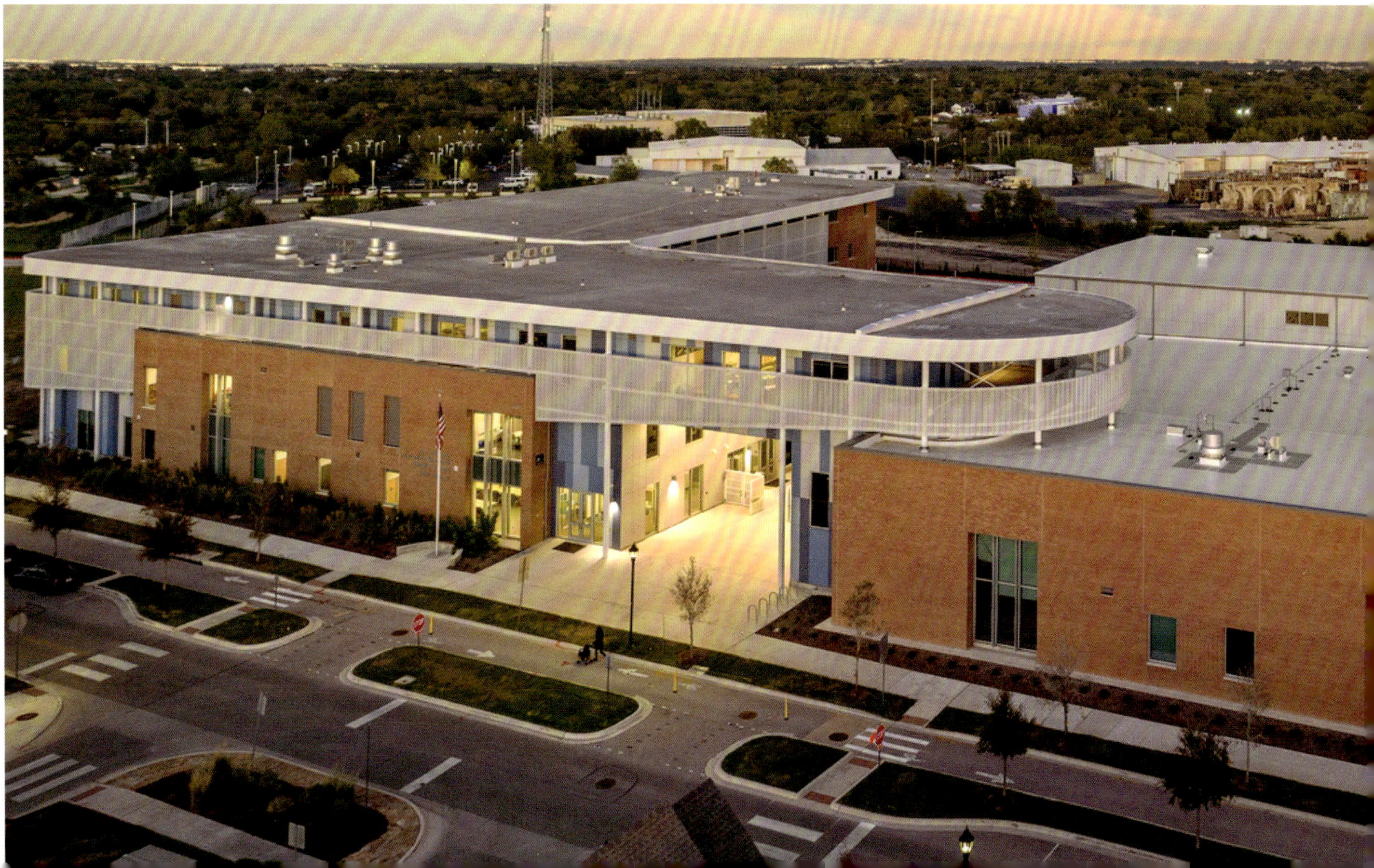

INTEGRATION

Austin Independent School District gathered a diverse group of consultants to fit the main building, gymnasium, tennis courts, and sports fields on the odd-shaped site and make them easily accessible to the surrounding neighborhoods. Landscape architects, civil engineers, recreation planners, and architects came together to master plan the campus and create a seamless neighborhood hub. The main welcoming portal connects to the neighborhood promenade, with green spaces embedded throughout. The landscape team carefully navigated proper field orientations, secure perimeters, site access, grading concerns, and site approach to create "hidden boundaries" between the community and district spaces. The layout and path make it easy for the school and neighborhood to share tennis, soccer, jogging, basketball, and meeting facilities. The interior design and architecture team coordinated building entries and door locations to safely partition the interior of the school for after-hours use.

Students quickly embraced the new campus. On any given day, the bike paths and sidewalks are filled. Most students walk, bike, or take mass transit to school. Soon after the school opened, administrators changed their policy and opened the courtyard, the school's "central park," before school hours, bringing energy and life to mornings on campus.

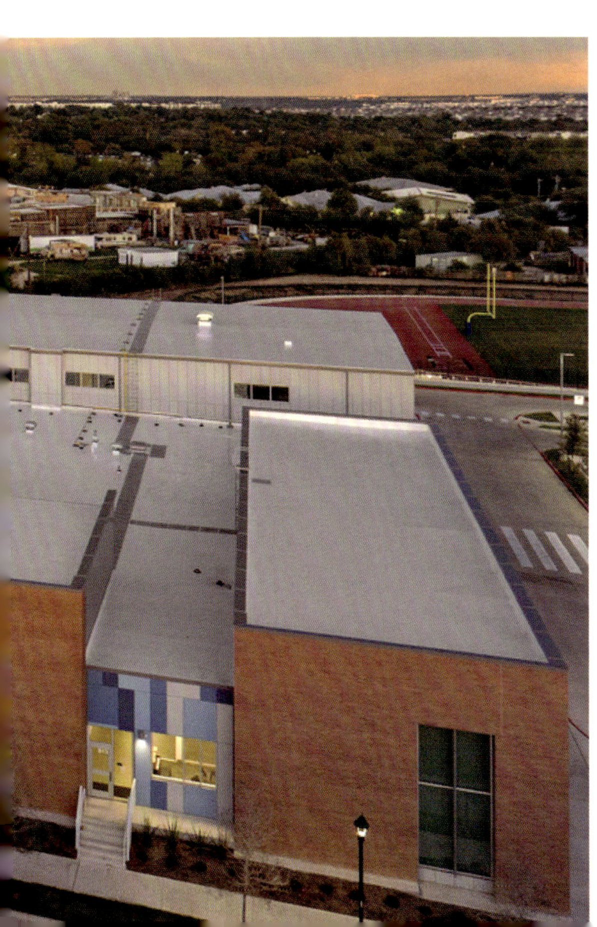

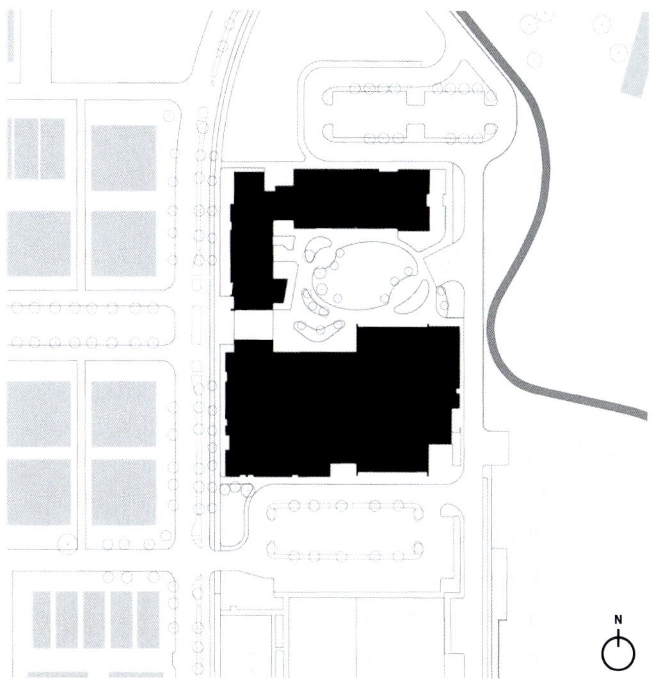

Performance

30%

OPERATIONAL CARBON EMISSIONS AVOIDED (mT/year)

501
625 436 0

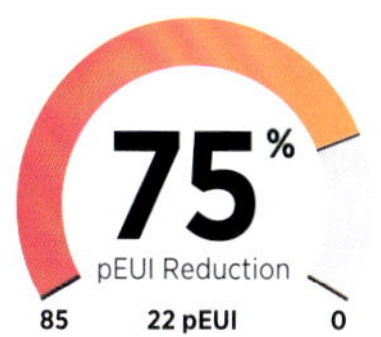

PREDICTED ENERGY USE INTENSITY (kBtu/sf/year)

Project	K12 | Public | 2022
Budget	$37 M
Scale	Large | 130,000 sf

Impact

800 Students Attend the School Daily

60% Water Use Reduction from Industry Baseline

100% of Rainwater Is Harvested and Used for Irrigation and Toilets

Recognition

3 Stars of Distinction Texas Association of School Administrators, 2024

LEED Gold

Wimberly Village Library Expansion

In drought-prone Texas Hill Country, a library rallies the community around water issues.

Wimberley Village Library is the first to incorporate a new state program for long-term water stewardship, focusing on water conservation and quality while serving as a community laboratory and educational resource.

Wimberley Village | Wimberley, TX

NO MORE

CONTEXT

Water is the lifeblood of Texas Hill Country. Thirteen rivers have their headwaters there, and for centuries Texans have understood the critical importance of protecting them. As the population of Hill Country has grown, pressures on water supplies have too. Town leaders recognized the opportunity to leverage a library expansion project as a platform for teaching water conservation. Rooted in an integrated water management approach called One Water, the design revolves around water both conceptually and practically, addressing water security while educating the community.

OUTCOME

Drawing on Wimberley's history as a trading post at the junction of the Blanco River and Cypress Creek, the building and site concepts centered on the notion of confluence, bringing people together. The building was sited and shaped to preserve mature live oak and elm trees and allow water to flow through the site naturally. Two single-pitched roofs define the reading room while guiding and directing stormwater to prominently displayed tanks. All water is managed on site, with bioretention basins and swales doubling as natural playgrounds. The new building connects with the old to create a facility to serve the community's future.

"In Hill Country, it often seems we are either in drought or we have a flood. It's one or the other, and it makes us very serious about water... The library is very focused on educating everybody about what we have done with water, so they can do it, too."

Aileen Edgington, District Board Trustee, Wimberley Village Library

BEFORE

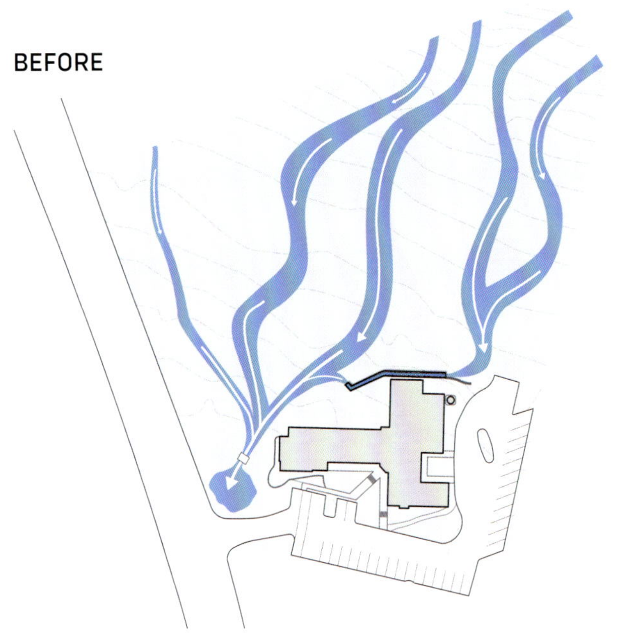

AFTER

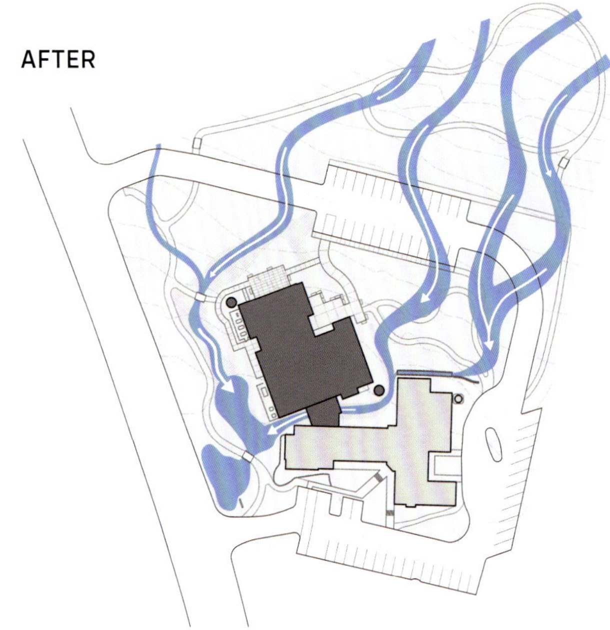

LIBRARY EXPANSION

"BRIDGE"

EXISTING LIBRARY

FRAMEWORK FOR DESIGN EXCELLENCE

DESIGN FOR INTEGRATION

The expansion is offset from the original building, a nod to the confluence of two local rivers, and nestled among mature, large-canopied oak and elm trees.

DESIGN FOR RESOURCES

Planning conversations about carbon and adaptive reuse led to the choice to reuse the existing library and reduce the addition footprint.

DESIGN FOR WATER

Water strategies make the most of every drop, with single-pitched roof, above-ground cisterns, on-site stormwater management, drought-tolerant planting, retention basins, bioswales, and nature playgrounds.

DESIGN FOR DISCOVERY

The library board wanted a “learning tool for the community” to teach sustainability through “on display” solar panels, rainwater collection, stormwater strategies, native vegetation, and daylight harvesting.

INTEGRATION

Architects and landscape architects worked with community leaders to notch, shift, and rotate the building to find the best combination that saved trees and preserved the natural water flow. The small structure linking the existing building with the expansion would have created a dam; instead, the team designed it as a bridge, allowing the water to run below a shared space with a quiet sitting area. Landscape architects helped develop a plan to move a road to the perimeter of the property, saving several trees. Retaining walls were installed at existing trees to protect the root zones and native grade, while still accommodating the stormwater biofiltration ponds. The single-sloped roofs that define the expansion's visual presence also direct stormwater runoff into the rainwater cisterns for capture and reuse in toilet flushing and irrigation systems. Bioswales were built at the low end of the site to retain and treat stormwater before it leaves the site.

At every step, designers focused on the light touch. Native and existing plant materials were preserved and enhanced with minimal new plantings. Considering the region's rapidly shifting needs, the site design and building expansion allows for future phases. The expansion is a transitional facility that can grow and evolve with future needs, while respecting and telling the story of the local environment.

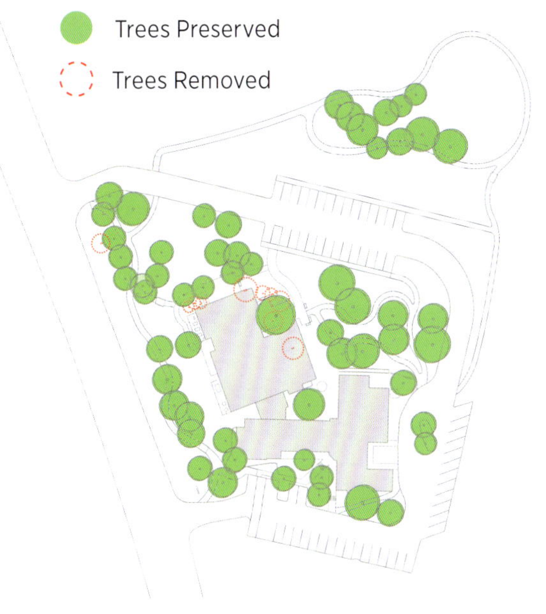

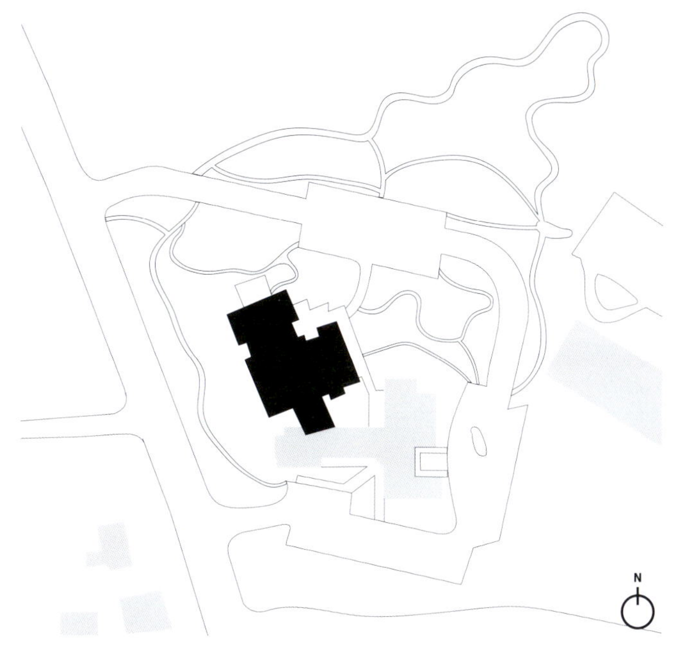

Performance

47% EMBODIED CARBON EMISSIONS AVOIDED (mT)

523 | 244 | 279 | 0

83% OPERATIONAL CARBON EMISSIONS AVOIDED (mT/year)

30 | 25 | 5 | 0

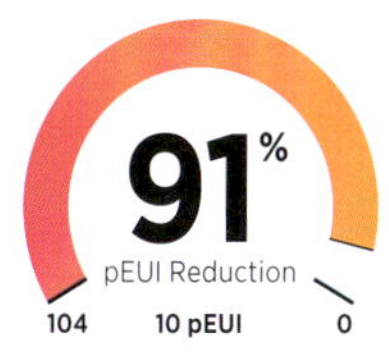

PREDICTED ENERGY USE INTENSITY (kBtu/sf/year)

Met the AIA Commitment 80% THRESHOLD at the time of design

Project	Civic | Library | 2024
Budget	$5.5 M
Scale	Small | 17,300 sf

Impact

113 Existing Trees

91% Existing Trees Preserved

10K Gallon Rain-Harvesting System for Irrigation and Toilet Fixtures

Recognition

COTE Award AIA Orange County, 2024
Honor Award AIA Orange County, 2024

Roosevelt High School

A historic campus modernization steeped in social justice.

L.A.'s Boyle Heights community feared that modernizing Roosevelt High School would dilute its civil rights legacy. Instead, the community-led redesign tells their story, consolidating hard-won gains in educational equity and setting the stage for future transformation.

Los Angeles Unified School District | Los Angeles, CA

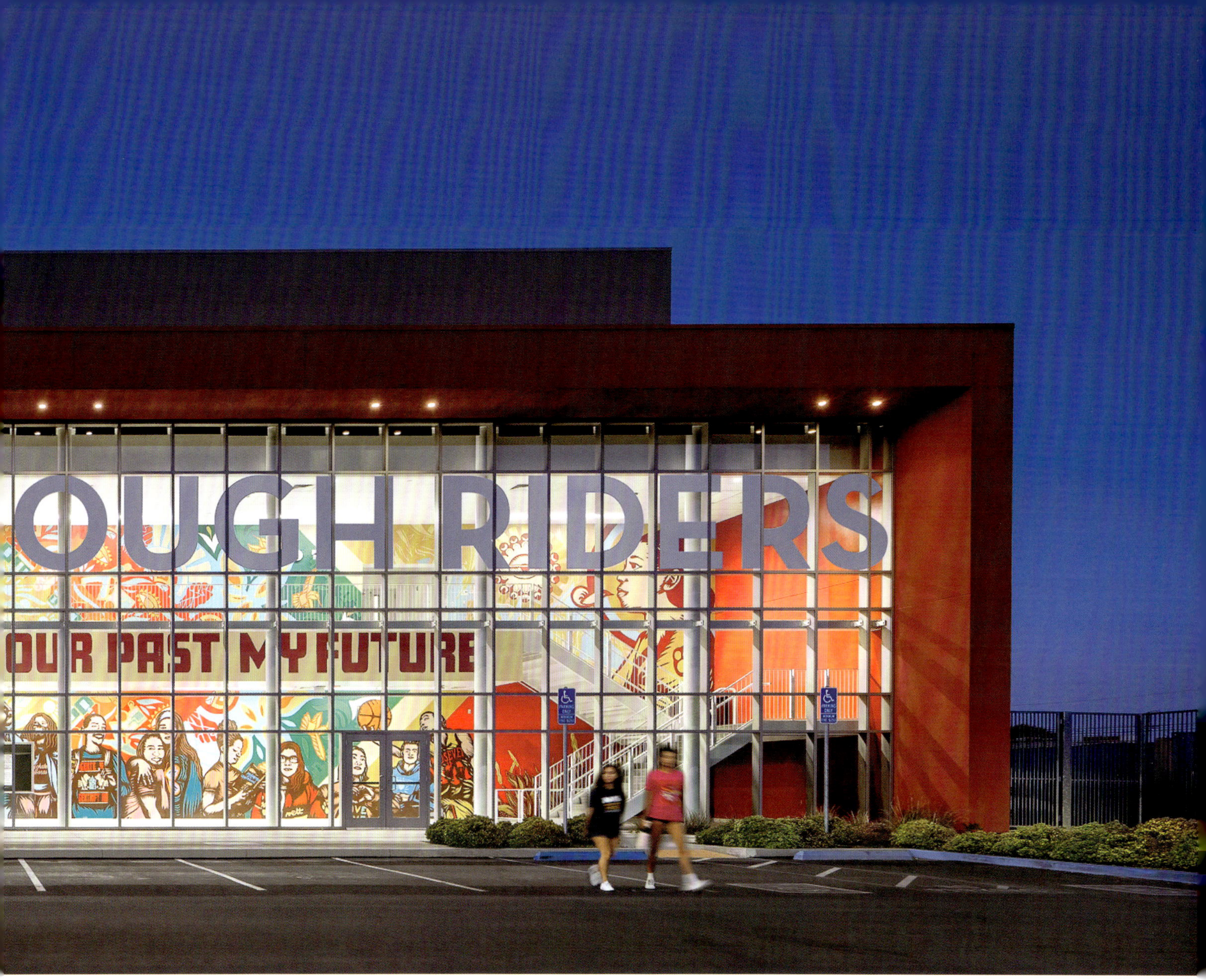
OUGH RIDERS
OUR PAST MY FUTURE

THEODORE
CHUMASH NATION

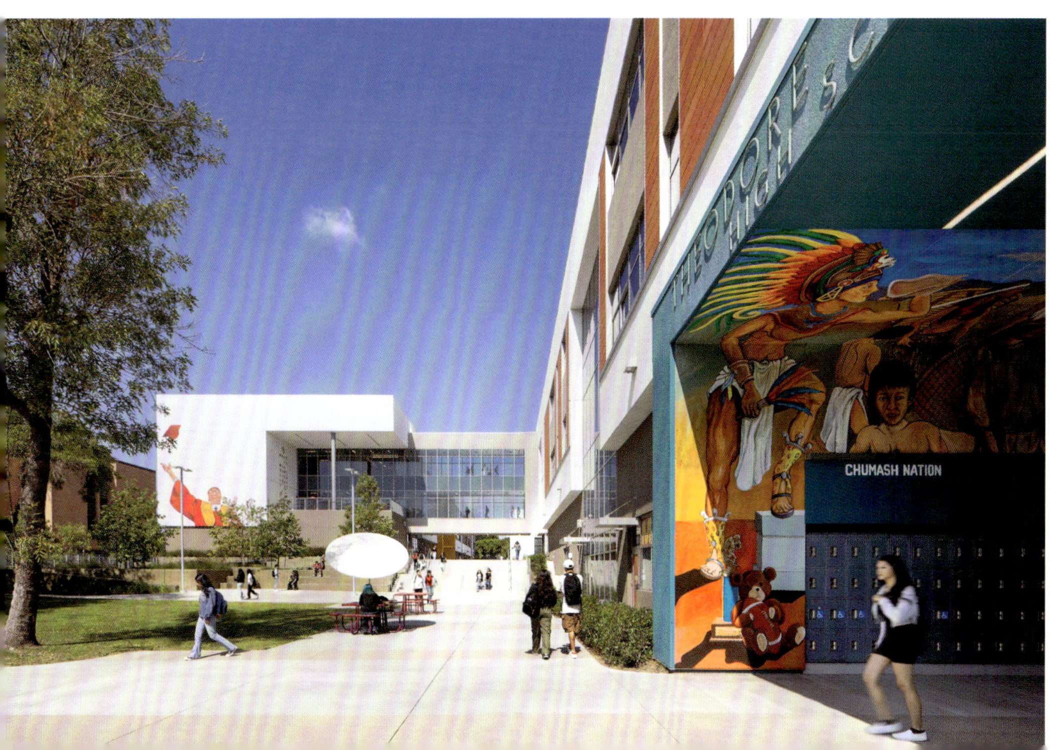

CONTEXT

Roosevelt High School is a cornerstone of Boyle Heights, a neighborhood known for its rich multicultural history and commitment to social justice. The school's identity is deeply tied to the 1968 East L.A. Blowouts, when Chicano students staged a historic walkout to demand educational equity. Community members who had seen their heritage marginalized over the years were wary the modernization would erase its legacy. Designers worked closely with trusted Roosevelt alumni, but the collaboration was tested when the auditorium, a pivotal site in the protests that many people wanted to preserve, was found to be structurally unsound. After lively discussions, the community found consensus on the project's goals to improve the quality of spaces throughout the campus.

OUTCOME

Boyle Heights' legacy of social justice is embedded in every element of the modernized campus. Inspired by the original East L.A. street grid, designers reorganized the site to be intuitive and accessible, with a grand, modern welcoming portal. Four new buildings bring Roosevelt's academic programs in line with the region's top campuses, fulfilling the promise of the 1968 protests. Outdoor terraces support diverse preferences and learning styles, offering each student a sense of belonging. A Japanese Garden of Peace, originally built in the '30s, was relocated and redesigned with input from a renowned Japanese garden landscape architect with ties to the Boyle Heights community. A three-story classroom building preserves the shape, scale, and lines of the demolished auditorium, while new murals document the community's history.

"The collaboration between LAUSD and LPA's integrated team has resulted in a community-focused, high-performance campus, while working within a system that requires a sensitive balance of competing priorities, budget challenges, educational goals, and facility stewardship."

Alix Walsh O'Brien **FAIA** Deputy Director of Facilities, Planning & Development, Los Angeles Unified School District

Before

After

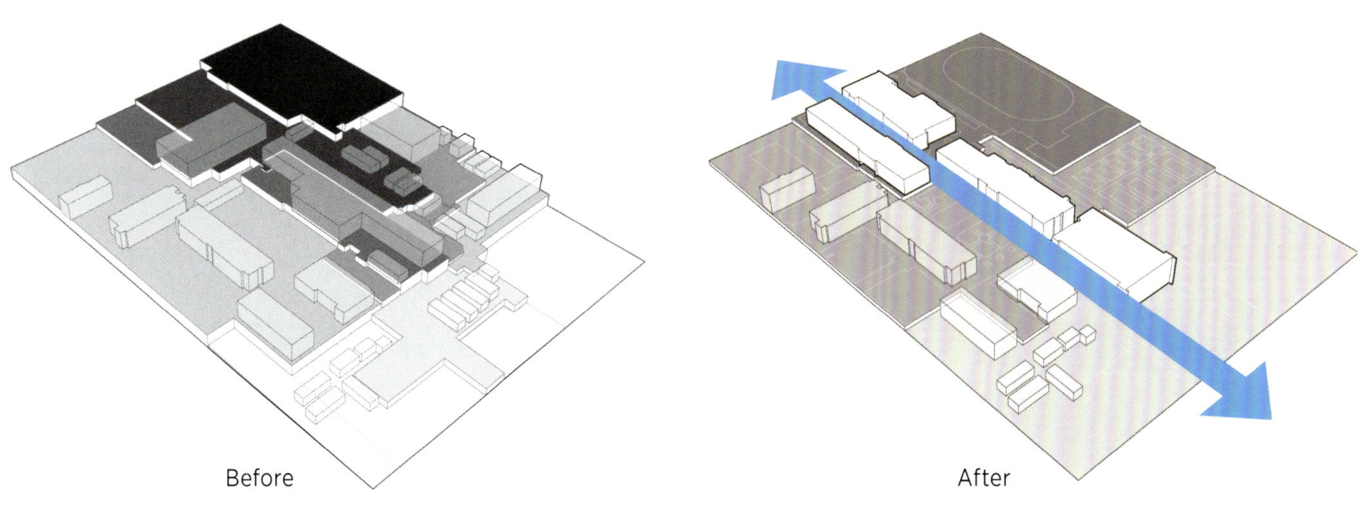

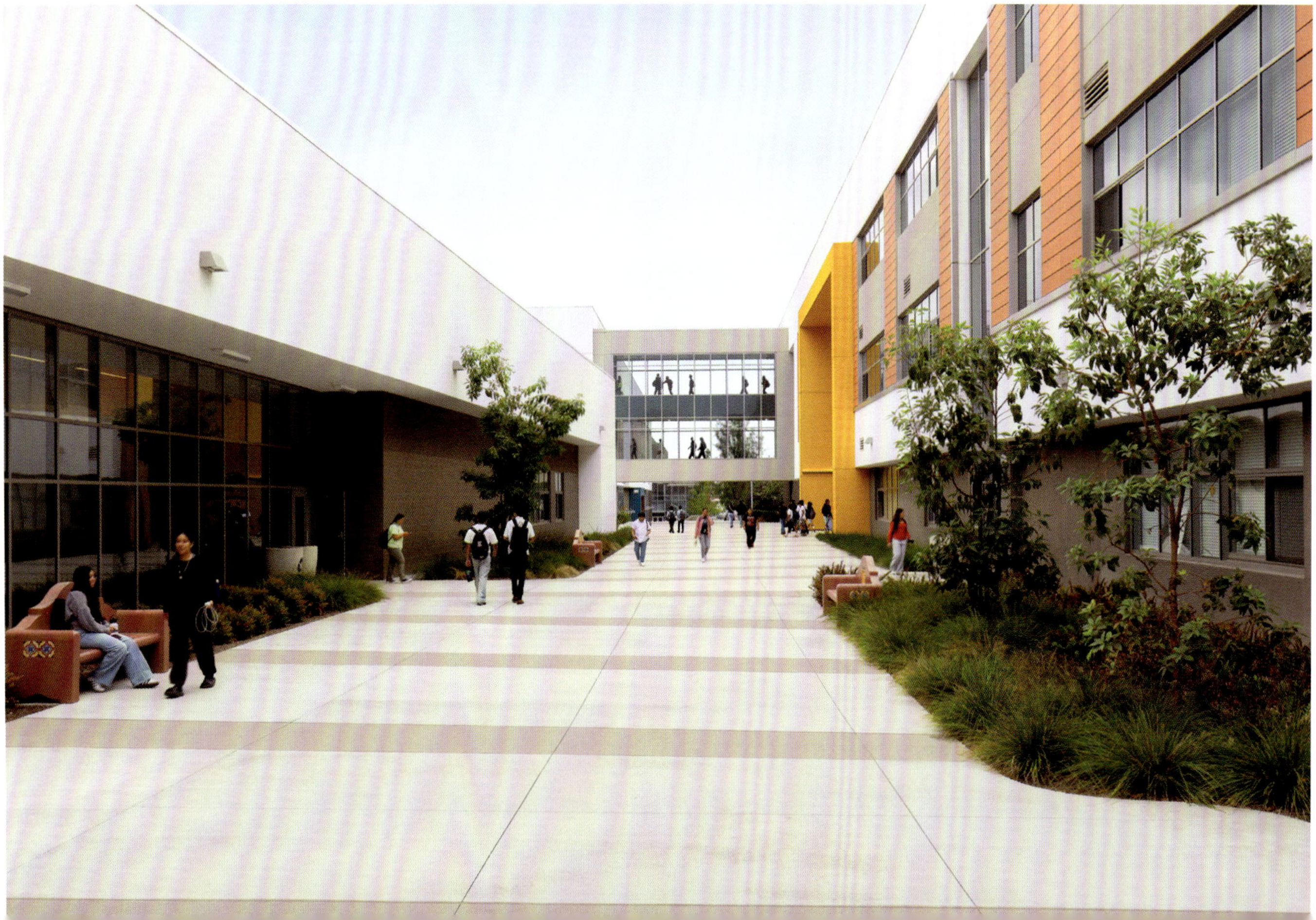

INTEGRATION

Before modernization, Roosevelt was a campus divided by several grade changes and inaccessible paths, posing significant barriers for students with disabilities and creating a fractured, inefficient environment for everyone. With a focus on universal design, civil engineers and landscape architects worked with designers, educators, and community leaders throughout the design process, searching for elements to make the campus more accessible and inclusive. Early discussions about the school's history focused designers on the idea of restoring the campus' historic axis, a simple promenade that once connected different buildings. As a result, the maze of buildings at multiple levels was replaced with four buildings on two levels, with a singular promenade linking academic, cultural, and athletic zones. The fifteen-foot elevation change was an opportunity to gain volume in ground-floor labs and create privacy for the Japanese Garden. Rather than moving soil to level the site, the landscape architects, designers, and engineers built an amphitheater into the slope, and a sky bridge was designed to symbolically connect past and future.

At each step, landscape architects added elements to support diversity and inclusion. Special-education classrooms open into the Japanese Garden, giving students easy access to restorative environments. The work on the garden drew everyone together, helping to create a direct link to the past, present, and future. A public process to select muralists elevated local artists and gave the people of Boyle Heights a direct role in telling their story.

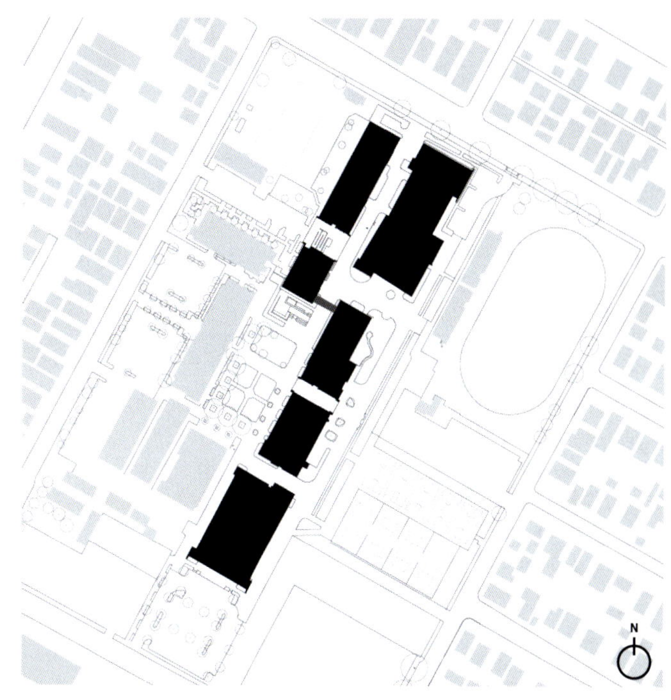

Performance

OPERATIONAL CARBON EMISSIONS AVOIDED
(mT/year)

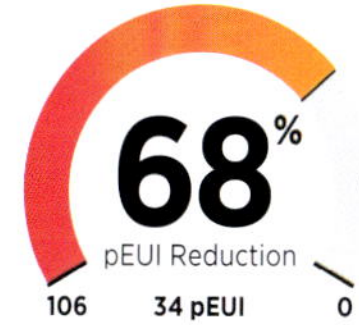

PREDICTED ENERGY USE INTENSITY
(kBtu/sf/year)

Project	K12 | Public | 2024
Budget	$150 M
Scale	Large | 250,000 sf

Impact

3 Murals Painted by Three Local Artists

7K Square-Foot Wellness Center / Health Clinic Supports the Local Community

5K Square-Foot Japanese Garden Celebrates Local Diversity

Recognition — **Merit Award** AIA California/CASH, 2025

Britton Middle School

Creating a new gateway for a growing downtown.

A transparent, two-story swirl of student life plays many roles for a school and a Northern California community.

Morgan Hill Unified School District | Morgan Hill, CA

"The new innovative and beautiful student union is an extension of downtown Morgan Hill. This project is something that everyone involved can be proud of, knowing they played a key role in its outcome."

Jackie Schaefer, Morgan Hill USD Bond Program Director

CONTEXT

The site chosen for Britton Middle School's new student union, an empty lot on the edge of the campus, sits on a highly visible corner at a key intersection at the entrance to downtown Morgan Hill, a rural bedroom community south of San Jose. The school has been a touchpoint for generations of local families, and local leaders made it clear in early discussions that they hoped the new facility would create a welcoming, defining building for downtown and serve as a community gathering spot. For Morgan USD, the student union was the last—and most visible—piece of a campus-wide transformation, and they wanted a "crown jewel" to serve as a model for future campuses.

OUTCOME

To create a strong local presence and extend the walkable downtown, the two-story building was moved right next to the sidewalk. The tall windows of the café and media center, shaded by a mass timber roof, is one of the first buildings visitors see as they enter downtown. The interior spaces are interconnected with glass walls, and a study pod appears to float in the space. A street-side entrance helps make the open hall a popular venue for a wide variety of public events, from town hall meetings to youth mariachi concerts. The street-front approach also freed space on the campus side of the building for outdoor learning and activity spaces, while preserving views of the surrounding mountains.

FRAMEWORK FOR DESIGN EXCELLENCE

DESIGN FOR EQUITABLE COMMUNITIES

Developed in a joint-use partnership, the student union doubles as an after-hours space for community events accessed via a secure, street-facing public entry.

DESIGN FOR ENERGY

Sustainability is on display throughout the all-electric building, which uses solar fins, sunshades, ceiling fans, operable walls, and windows to reduce energy demand.

DESIGN FOR WELL-BEING

Natural ventilation improves air quality in 100% of regularly occupied indoor spaces. Landscaping designed around the social needs of middle schoolers provides choice, a sense of belonging, and views to a natural landmark.

DESIGN FOR RESOURCES

A large, mass-timber overhang sequesters carbon while shading a richly programmed outdoor balcony and courtyard, reducing the need for enclosed space.

ESSENTIALS

INTEGRATION

The tall, open building that would become the student union's emblematic connection to the community presented an array of challenges. Mechanical and structural engineers struggled to create the type of welcoming environment envisioned by the designers.

The big break came from a member of the structural team, who proposed moving most of the large mechanical equipment over a one-story support space, simplifying the seismic risk-reduction strategy for the main building. That moment led to the glulam beam roof structure, which became the building's chief identifier and unifying element, providing warmth and a connection to nature. The roof extends to create a value-added outdoor space on the campus side of the building. Landscape architects activated the covered area with spaces for learning and social activities, working with researchers to provide an array of environments for a neurodiverse student body. Minimizing the mechanical system also left the roof open for the possibility of adding PV panels in the future.

All the elements support the lighting design, which turns the building into a work of art. The seismic bracing strategy accommodates a series of indirect and direct lighting fixtures, casting light and shadow across the building, unobstructed by mechanical systems. The study pod appears as a glowing presence. Programmable color LEDs light the vertical shade fins and tall windows, turning the facade into a nightly billboard of light that brings the student union to life.

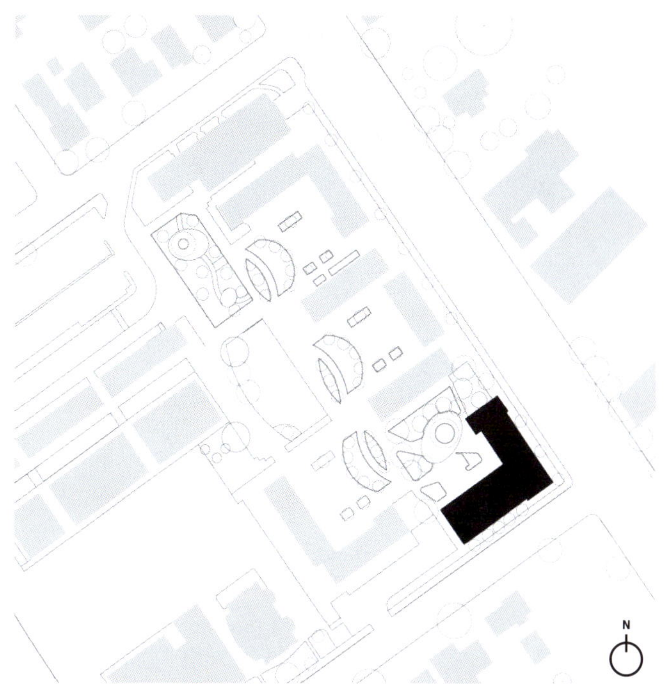

Performance

31 %

39

111 72 0

OPERATIONAL CARBON EMISSIONS AVOIDED (mT/year)

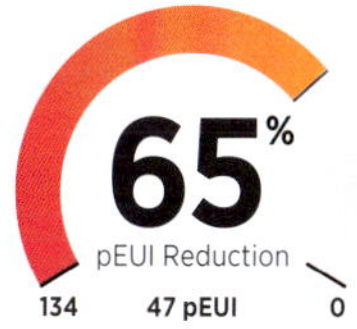

PREDICTED ENERGY USE INTENSITY (kBtu/sf/year)

Project	K12 | Public | 2024
Budget	$29 M
Scale	Medium | 32,000 sf

Impact

100% Electrified

100% of Regularly Occupied Spaces Have Access to Natural Ventilation

24 Years for the Project's Site Design to Become Carbon Neutral

Recognition: Merit Award, AIA California/CASH, 2025

LIGHTING

STRUCTURAL AND LIGHTING TEAMS COLLABORATED TO INTEGRATE LIGHTING FIXTURES THAT SPOTLIGHT THE FACILITY AND GIVE IT A DRAMATIC PRESENCE AT NIGHT.

Sustainability at Scale

We design for sustainability on every project, regardless of budget or scale. Each scale requires a different approach, while measuring performance, quantifying value, and leaning on the expertise of an integrated team.

Edwards Lifesciences Headquarters

Awakening a giant of ecological responsibility.

Starting with a parking garage and growing into a half-million-square-foot campus expansion, LPA's relationship with Edwards Lifesciences tracks their evolution as global leaders in corporate sustainability.

Edwards Lifesciences | Irvine, CA

CONTEXT

Edwards lacked sustainable objectives when we began our collaboration in 2011. We helped them change that by repeatedly demonstrating the measurable value of sustainable design. Over thirteen years and two master plans, we witnessed their evolution into an ESG pacesetter. Starting with a PV-topped parking garage that included the largest green wall in North America at the time, they began to see how quality of life and energy reduction produced bottom-line results. By 2018, with a ten-acre expansion, they had set ambitious goals for water and waste, and committed to carbon neutrality by 2030. Working as an integrated team, we guided Edwards through a series of envelope-pushing projects, including two net-zero and LEED Platinum entry buildings and three LEED Gold buildings that support office, labs, conferencing, and food service.

OUTCOME

The campus redevelopment achieved Edwards' goals while improving environmental performance at every step. Corridors, stairs, and connecting walkways are pulled to the exterior, minimizing energy consumption and creating spaces for casual collisions that encourage innovation. Designers moved program areas outdoors, into shaded gathering spaces and planted roof decks, reducing embodied carbon while creating rooftop space to add photovoltaic canopies. To enhance well-being, the design includes a landscape full of drought-tolerant plants, with its bioretention areas, modular wetlands, and the largest cistern system in Orange County.

Edwards is now on pace to achieve its goal of carbon neutrality by 2030 and is routinely honored with "most sustainable" and "most ethical" accolades.

"There's sophistication and elegance in how these spaces interact, the way people move through and can see each other at different levels. This team took it all the way. Great design AND great sustainability—weaving those two together is important, and this project did a great job of that."

AIA OC COTE Award Jury

INTEGRATION

Edwards, which views sustainability as critical to its mission of "improving quality of life around the world," challenged designers to "show the PV." Rather than hiding the panels, integrated teams looked to make the energy infrastructure an integral part of the campus' design language. Panels are installed creatively throughout the campus, including in shading devices or subtly peeking over the edges of buildings. Several building entrances are highlighted by a thin ridge of PV panels cantilevering past the lip of a silver, knife-edge canopy. In this exposed position, the brittle panels are vulnerable to wind forces, but structural and electrical engineers carefully studied tolerances and devised a concealed backbone to tie the PV securely to the structure and make the visual statement possible.

Similar collaboration was required for the shaded gathering spaces and parking canopies throughout the site. Normally, the underside of PV panels is a tangle of wires. In this case, architects and engineers collaborated to thread wires through hollow steel members, creating a clean appearance that belies its complexity. The effort has paid off. After years of progress, the PV panels proudly on display contribute to a campus-wide system totaling 2.25 mW—a defining achievement for one of the largest customer-owned renewable energy systems in California.

ELECTRICAL ENGINEERING

THROUGHOUT THE CAMPUS, ENGINEERS AND DESIGNERS EMBEDDED PV PANELS IN SHADE STRUCTURES, PUTTING THE SOLAR STRATEGY ON DISPLAY.

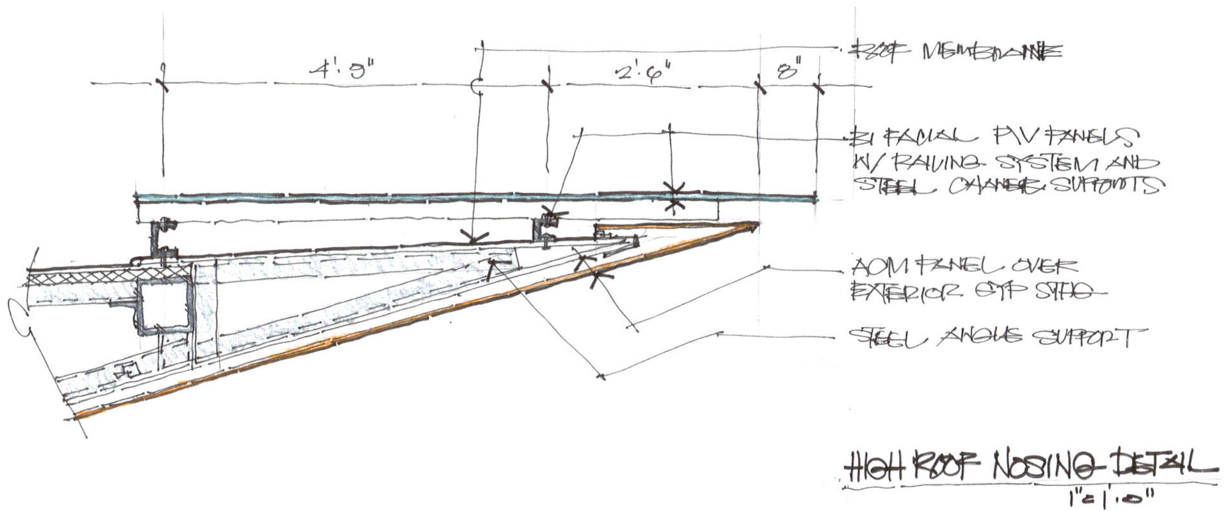

STRUCTURAL ENGINEERING

TO CANTILEVER A THIN LIP OF PV PANELS OVER A CANOPY, STRUCTURAL ENGINEERS AND DESIGNERS DEVISED A CONCEALED BACKBONE TO TIE THE PV SECURELY TO THE STRUCTURE.

FRAMEWORK FOR DESIGN EXCELLENCE

DESIGN FOR INTEGRATION

A campus of office, lab, conference, dining, and pavilion buildings are connected by a network of outdoor elevated walkways, bridges, and social spaces to maximize chance encounters and strengthen innovation.

DESIGN FOR ECOSYSTEMS

Ten acres of asphalt is replaced by a diverse landscape that treats 100% of stormwater, mitigates heat island effect, and adds 560 trees to serve as habitat.

DESIGN FOR WATER

Drought-tolerant planting cuts site water use by 70%, with a 60,000-gallon rainwater-harvesting system, one of the largest in California, providing irrigation.

DESIGN FOR ENERGY

Buildings totaling over 500,000 sf achieved a 70% pEUI reduction from baseline, with two net-zero-energy consumers, and 2.25 mW of on-site PV.

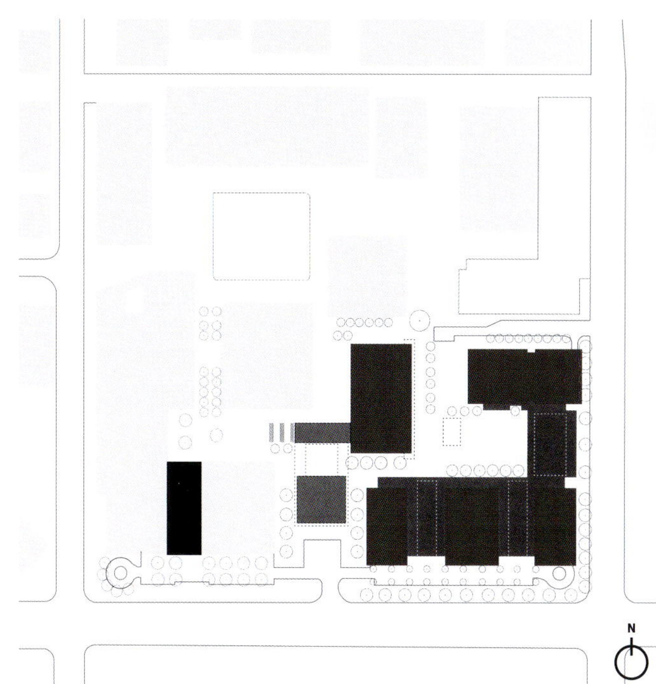

Performance

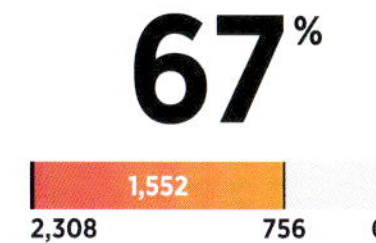

OPERATIONAL CARBON EMISSIONS AVOIDED
(mT/year)

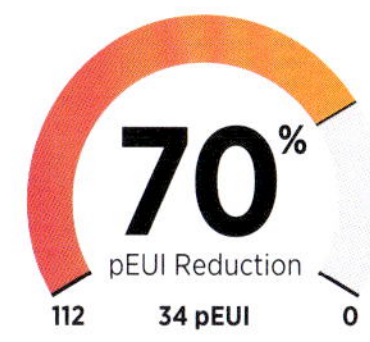

PREDICTED ENERGY USE INTENSITY
(kBtu/sf/year)

Met the AIA Commitment
70% THRESHOLD
at the time of design

Project	Workplace | Expansion | 2017–2023
Budget	Confidential
Scale	Large | 492,000 sf

Impact

4K Employees Campus-Wide

50% Above Seismic Building Code for Resilience

60K Gallon Rainwater-Harvesting System

Recognition

COTE Award AIA Orange County, 2022
Merit Award AIA Orange County, 2022
Award of Merit SCAOSC, 2021
Project of the Year ASCE OC, 2021
COTE Award AIA Orange County, 2017
Honor Award AIA Orange County, 2017
Interiors Merit Award AIA California, 2018
Merit Award ASLA SC, 2018
2 LEED Platinum, 3 LEED Gold

California State University, Northridge Recreation Center

Site, systems, and structure in sync.

When an expansive vision for student recreation hit space-constrained reality, designers focused on small details to deliver high performance and meet programming needs. Shaped through methodical iteration, the rec center's "folded" structure optimizes energy and materials while blending seamlessly into its suburban neighborhood.

CSU Northridge | Los Angeles, CA

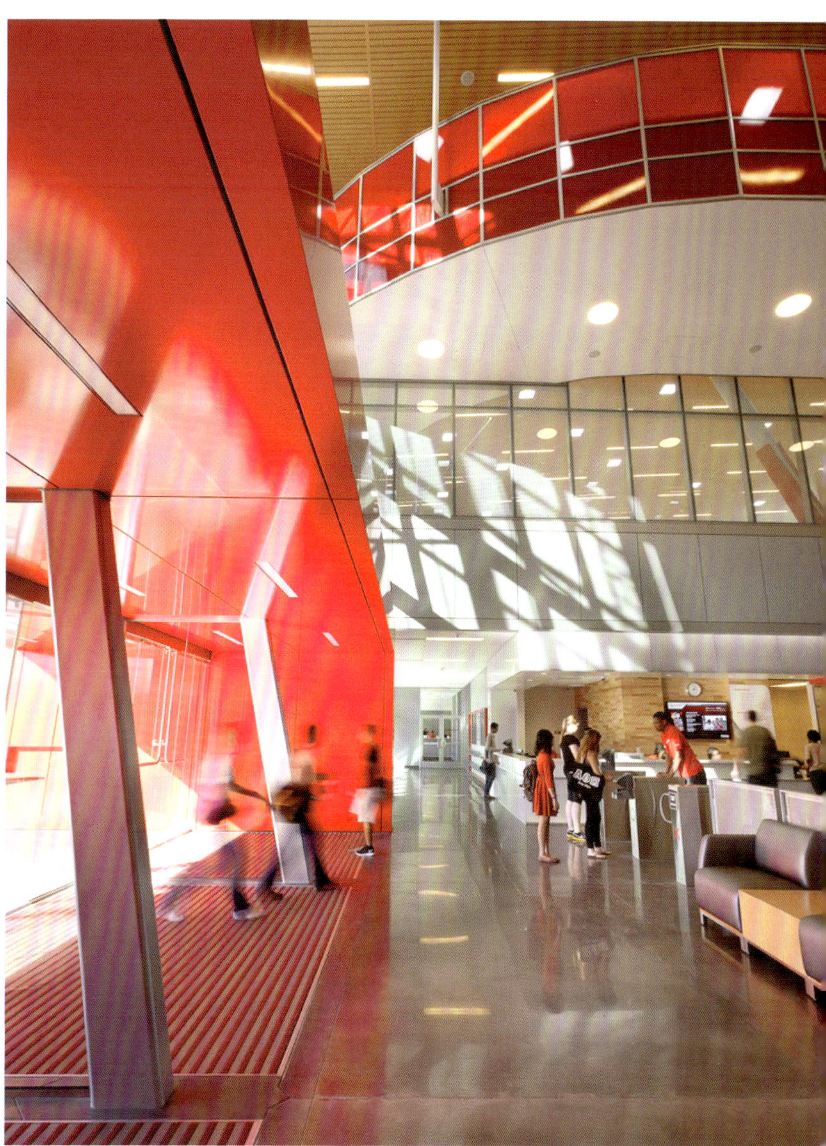

STUDENT

CONTEXT

An early adopter of large-scale solar power, drought resilience, and LEED, California State University, Northridge was already recognized as a "model sustainable campus." But it was going to be a challenge to bring high performance to the new recreation center, which was intended to change the paradigm of the evolving campus and keep students on campus longer. Administrators wanted to pack health and wellness options into a three-story building that barely fit on the narrow north-south site, which made the building highly susceptible to solar heat and glare. At the same time, school leaders wanted the building to maintain a low profile to blend with the local residential community.

> **"How do you design it in such a way that it's still aesthetically pleasing and functional? I think that integrated design and LPA was able to achieve that for us."**
>
> Debra Hammond, Executive Director, CSUN

OUTCOME

The site's constraints served as an unexpected catalyst for innovation. Using some of the first energy-modeling tools available, designers shaped the facades around a balance of shading and natural light and displacement ventilation. To fit in with low-slung neighbors to the east and west, an intensive right-sizing effort significantly reduced the building's height and use of steel. Designers approached the narrow building like an airplane fuselage, fitting the structural, electrical, and mechanical systems into a compact space. The optimized design folds together like a paper clip, shortening the building's height by eight feet while accommodating a forty-six-foot rock-climbing wall, a running track, and a three-court gymnasium. Roof overhangs and a series of vertical perforated metal panels reduce the solar heat gain and glare by 50%.

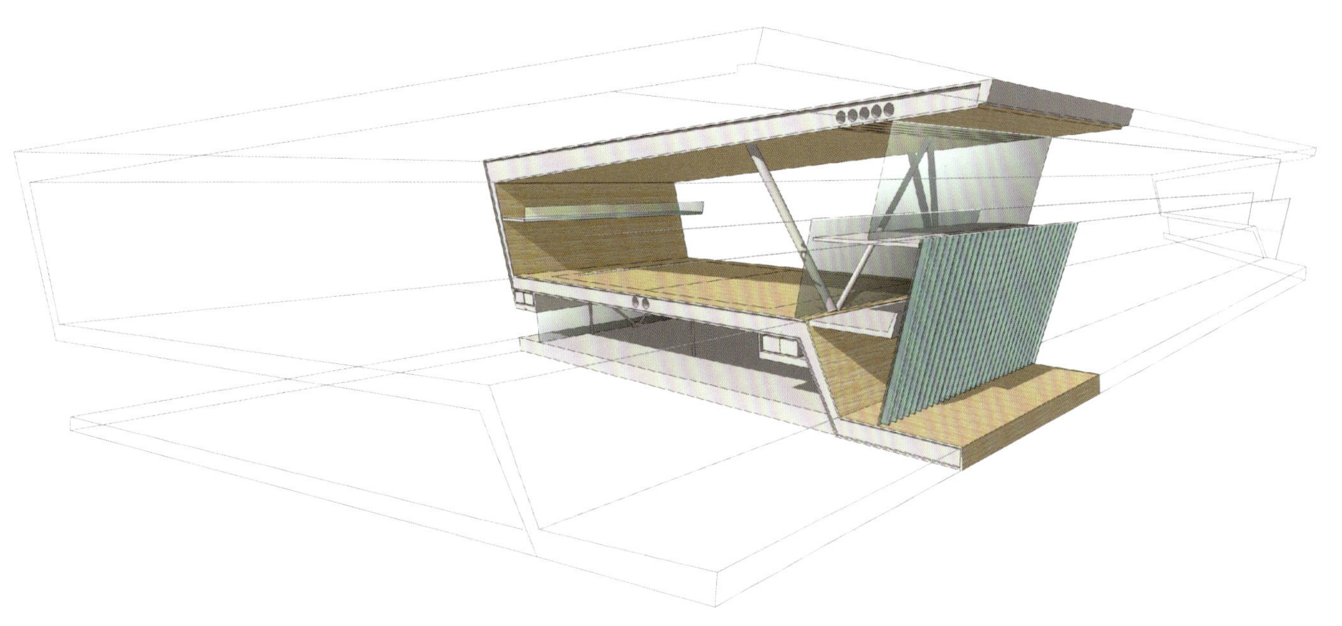

INTEGRATION

In the wake of the 1994 Northridge earthquake, the facility needed to meet strict new seismic codes. Structural and mechanical engineers worked from the start to accommodate the structural requirements while reducing materials, lowering the building's profile, and maximizing performance. A traditional brace frame system would have been a conventional choice, but its bulk risked overwhelming the site. Instead, the structural engineers designed an innovative inverted tripod system to support the elevated gyms. Formed from canted diagonal buckling-restrained braces, the multi-story tripods enhance seismic resilience while adding lateral stiffness, restraining the "folded" building form's natural tendency to "unfold" under its own weight. This creative approach reduced the amount of steel required—and building height. A suspended running track winds through the tripod structure high above the gyms.

The mechanical engineers helped the cause by keeping equipment off the roof, which lowered the building's center of gravity and enabled ductwork to be concealed between floors. This configuration supported an efficient displacement ventilation system, cooling only the occupied areas of the high-volume spaces. The cleared roof also made room for solar tubes, which flood the gyms with natural light. With walls and ceilings free of mechanical equipment, designers clad the gym interiors in repurposed-wood athletic flooring, creating a vibrant, light-filled environment that reflects CSUN's sustainable ethos.

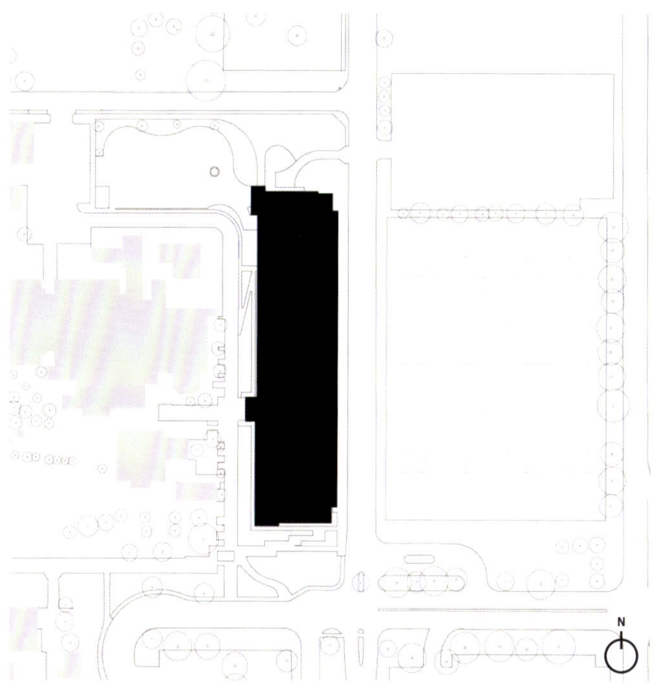

Performance

42% OPERATIONAL CARBON EMISSIONS AVOIDED (mT/year)

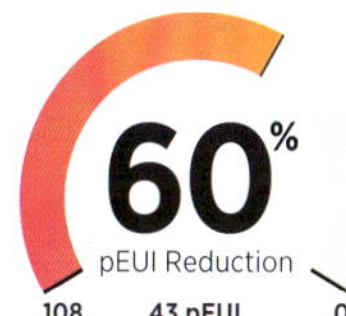

PREDICTED ENERGY USE INTENSITY (kBtu/sf/year)

Project	Higher Education | 2012
Budget	$50 M
Scale	Large | 123,000 sf

Impact

100% Funded by Student Fees

100% of Large Assembly Spaces Utilize Thermal Displacement HVAC Systems

90% of Building Occupants Have Access to Natural Daylight and Quality Views

Recognition

Merit Award AIA Orange County, 2010

Design and Vision Award COTE AIA San Diego, 2012

CAE / AIA National Excellence in Design Award 2023

LEED Gold

STRUCTURAL ENGINEERING

AN INVERTED TRIPOD SYSTEM WITH DIAGONAL LEGS EFFICIENTLY PROVIDES LATERAL SUPPORT FOR THE BUILDING WHILE LEAVING ROOM FOR A RUNNING TRACK.

Los Medanos College Kinesiology Campus

Budget efficiency yields performance gains.

Designers' suggestion to combine two complementary projects unlocked budget, performance, and programmatic synergies. The resulting pair of campus buildings elevates wellness and social cohesion at a community college.

Contra Costa Community College District | Pittsburg, CA

"LPA's design exceeded our expectations of what our budget could support... Both buildings embody principles of sustainable design in a way that nurtures future-ready, socially responsible leaders."

Ines Zildzic, Vice Chancellor, Facilities Planning and Construction

CONTEXT

After forty-five years in operation, Pittsburg, California's only higher-education institution was struggling to keep students on campus. Spurred by research connecting student engagement and academic success, the community college enlisted LPA to design a student union. Seeing synergies between the project and a separate kinesiology project, designers suggested combining the two into a single complex devoted to wellness and student life. Designers shared data supporting the idea that a larger scale would afford them better-quality materials, a higher degree of energy performance, and a greater impact on students.

OUTCOME

The complex creates a "living room for students" connected to a fitness hub by an activated, connective landscape. The holistic approach leverages the relationship between wellness and student life, with fitness activities prominently displayed through windows, learning and event spaces that blend indoors and outdoors, and student-centric support spaces. The combined scope helped pay for more resilient materials, more efficient mechanical systems, and an ultra-efficient building envelope, while the larger scope made drought-tolerant landscaping a more integral part of the project. Together with passive strategies such as self-shading and daylighting, a PV array helped reduce energy use by 79% for the LEED Gold certified buildings.

INTEGRATION

The student union was envisioned as a "building in the round," transparently engaging the campus on all sides of the facility. For designers, this was a tough starting point for maximizing energy efficiency, with the south, west, and east interiors exposed to the sun. Working the problem, mechanical engineers and architects developed precise shading strategies for each facade, optimizing fenestration to reduce heat gain while maintaining daylighting and campus connectivity. Different types of fins were tested and revised—vertical, horizontal, wide, narrow—based on the exact sun angle.

At each step, the team balanced the potential for campus-making with opportunities to cut energy and lower costs. For the Kinesiology Complex, teams saw an opportunity to improve campus cohesion by mirroring and elevating the aesthetic of the adjacent gym. However, the preference for bulky rooftop air handlers, which are less costly and easier to maintain, clashed with the design goal. To hide the equipment, designers worked with the engineers to reorganize the building program. Interior private spaces were consolidated under a lower roof on the west side, creating room for mechanical units above. High-ceiling spaces were grouped together on the east side. The taller facade was then extended around the building to screen the rooftop units, completing an effect experienced across multiple buildings. Most people won't even know the more efficient equipment is there. But it will lower the facility's energy use and maintenance costs daily.

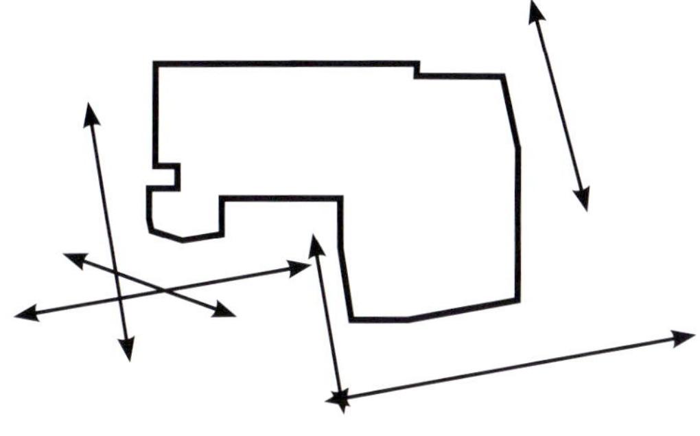

STUDENT UNION CONCEPT PLAN

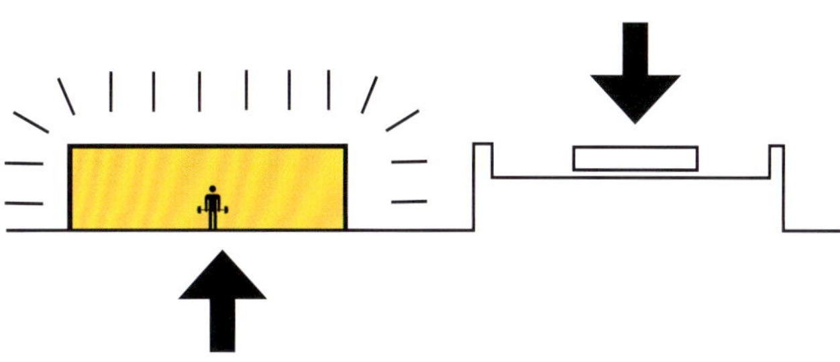

KINESIOLOGY CENTER CONCEPT SECTION

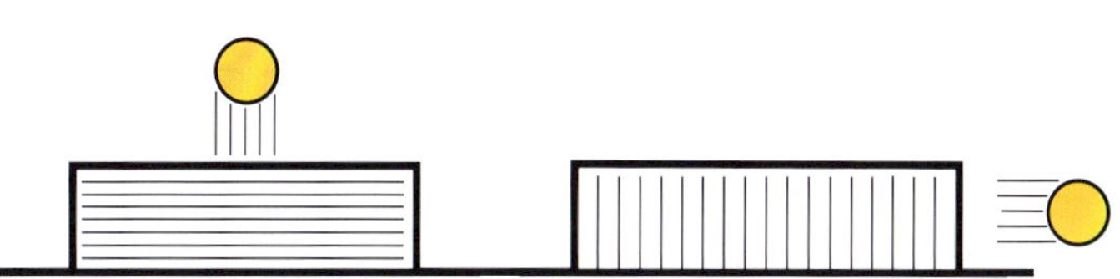

MOST EFFICIENT SHADING PER ORIENTATION

ENGINEERING

BUILDINGS WERE ORIENTED TO PROTECT INTERIORS FROM THE SUN WHILE MEETING CAMPUS GOALS.

FRAMEWORK FOR DESIGN EXCELLENCE

DESIGN FOR INTEGRATION

Stitches together the campus fabric with a connective, activated landscape and bridging materiality that links the original Brutalist concrete with the metal-and-glass palette of recent additions.

DESIGN FOR EQUITABLE COMMUNITIES

Provides a comprehensive campus life for underserved students, with an inclusive program of student-centric spaces for clubs, student government, and community.

DESIGN FOR ECOSYSTEMS

A network of outdoor programmed spaces connects students with nature. Terraced landscapes under a grove of trees create new habitats while treating 100% of rainwater.

DESIGN FOR ENERGY

Carefully sited, self-shading buildings use ultra-high-performing skin, efficient air-handling units, and on-site PV to reduce pEUI by 79% and meet the 2030 Commitment.

DESIGN FOR WELL-BEING

Infuses wellness into student life with social and active spaces to exert, stretch, lift, run, dance, meditate, and heal—all prominently displayed in bright, daylit spaces.

STUDENT UNION

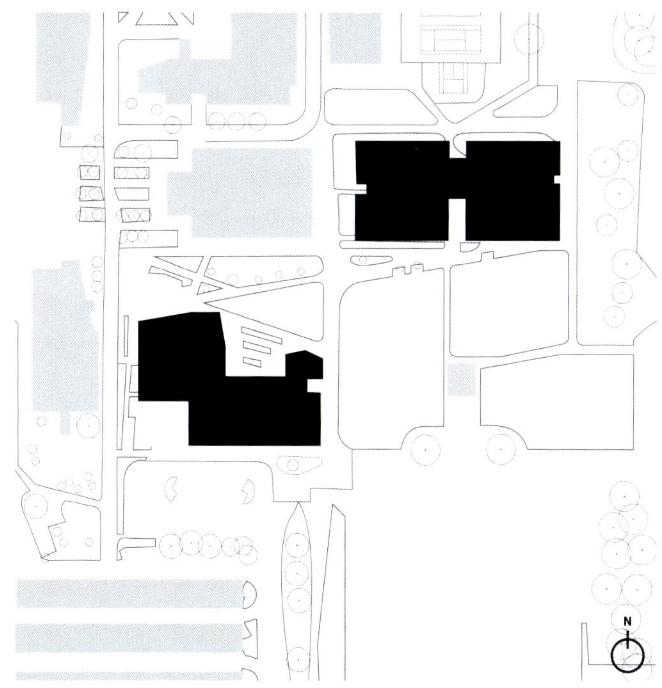

Performance

OPERATIONAL CARBON EMISSIONS AVOIDED
(mT/year)

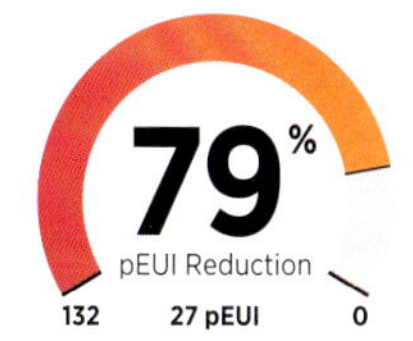

PREDICTED ENERGY USE INTENSITY
(kBtu/sf/year)

Met the AIA Commitment
70% THRESHOLD
at the time of design

Project	Higher Ed | Sport+Rec | Student Union | 2020
Budget	$43.5 M
Scale	Medium | 67,000 sf

Impact

100% of Education Spaces Have Access to Daylight

18% of Energy Consumption Offset by Renewable Energy

100% of Stormwater Treated on Site

Recognition

Honor Award AIA Silicon Valley, 2023
Sierra Merit Award ASLA Sierra Valley, 2022
Award of Honor CCFC, 2021
LEED Gold

Piedmont Hills High School Science & Life Skills Complex

A modest STEM village transcends its budget limitations.

Designers squeezed every bit of design out of ordinary, resilient materials, using passive strategies to do more with less at every turn.

East Side Union High School District | San Jose, CA

> "It's really hard to do these projects well, with tight budgets and lots of constraints, but any difficulty this team experienced is absolutely invisible in the final result."

AIA Silicon Valley Jury

CONTEXT

Piedmont Hills High School, located in the low-income area of East San Jose, has not shared in the success of Silicon Valley. For years, a large portion of the science program was inadequately housed in portable classrooms on an underutilized, sloping site at the south side of the campus. With students asking for more STEM opportunities, the school needed a new facility on a modest budget. The Science and Classroom Buildings presented an opportunity to set a new standard for educational spaces at the school. But with Bay Area construction costs at historic highs, efficiency was critical.

OUTCOME

The design leverages the Bay Area's mild climate to cut built square footage, bring learning outdoors, and reduce operating costs. Three buildings form a southwest edge to the campus. Cut into the existing slope, they define and shade an outdoor "science courtyard" where classes spill out through overhead doors. All circulation is exterior, with a whimsical ramp weaving among shade trees, collab pods, and an outdoor classroom to provide accessibility. Limited by cost to wood framing, designers used punched windows as a playful foil to the straightforward building forms, balancing daylight and heat gain. Individual HVAC controls and PVs helped reduce energy use by 72%.

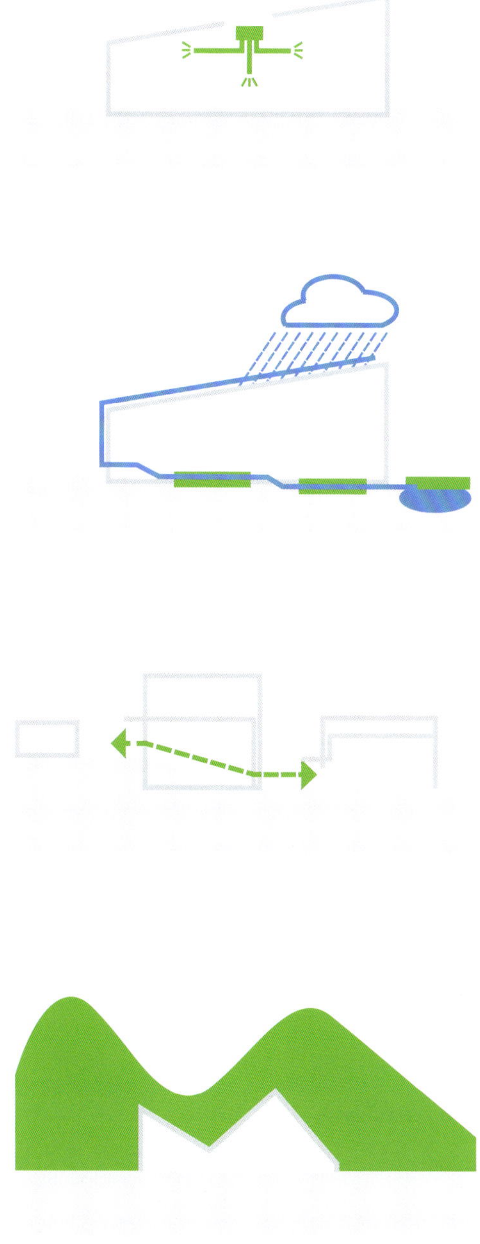

INTEGRATION

The site's steep slope was a formidable obstacle to connecting the buildings and realizing the school's programming goals within the budget constraints. Rather than leveling the terrain or installing an elevator, landscape architects and civil engineers developed alternatives, ultimately preserving the natural slope by connecting the different levels with the distinctive winding ramp and creating universal accessibility. Drought-resilient landscape and flow-through planters connect to the campus-wide rainwater drainage system and bioretention areas. The exterior circulation and ramps reduce the built space and promote an active campus.

Mechanical engineers collaborated with designers to organize the buildings and consolidate small, efficient mechanical systems above the prep spaces centered on the lower roofs between science classrooms. This arrangement reduced ductwork while preserving the building's full height and maximizing natural light. Perforated metal screens reveal glimpses of the efficient equipment, while aligning with the diagonal rooflines and blending seamlessly into the building's materiality and color palette. All elements work together to make the courtyard the focal point, the anchor to a new campus experience, connecting students to science and sustainability the moment they arrive.

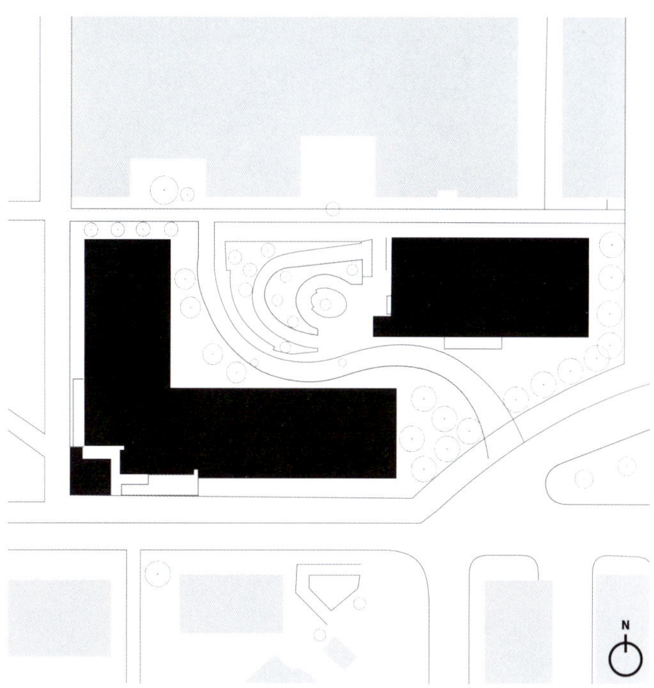

LANDSCAPE

LANDSCAPE ARCHITECTS AND CIVIL ENGINEERS COLLABORATED TO SCULPT THE SITE ON THIS SLOPED CAMPUS.

Performance

20%
96
461 365 0
EMBODIED CARBON EMISSIONS AVOIDED
(mT)

58%
49
84 35 0
OPERATIONAL CARBON EMISSIONS AVOIDED
(mT/year)

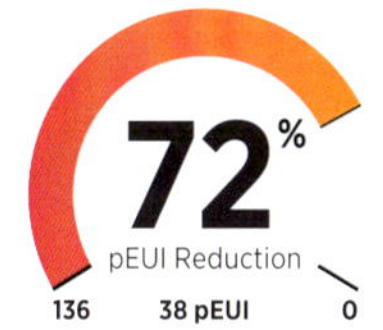

PREDICTED ENERGY USE INTENSITY
(kBtu/sf/year)

Met the AIA Commitment
70% THRESHOLD
at the time of design

Project	K-12 | Public | 2019
Budget	$9.62 M
Scale	Small | 15,742 sf

Impact

100% Active Design (No Elevators)

100% Wood Construction

46K Gallons of Potable Water Saved Each Year

Recognition

Honor Award AIA Silicon Valley, 2020
Honor Award AIA Central Valley, 2019
Divine Detail Award AIA Central Valley, 2019

Environmental Nature Center & Preschool

A net-positive campus teaches ecological stewardship.

The ENC was established to teach future generations to protect the natural world. Our work together over ten years helped them grow from a modular trailer to a 4.7-acre campus. These two small-scale projects elevate and embody ENC's mission.

Environmental Nature Center | Newport Beach, CA

B
Nature Preschool
The Frank and Joan Randall
ENC Nature Preschool Classrooms

FRAMEWORK FOR DESIGN EXCELLENCE

DESIGN FOR INTEGRATION

Site and climate data informed the placement, orientation, and design of the two buildings to immerse children in nature and achieve 100% natural ventilation.

DESIGN FOR ECOSYSTEMS

The design makes students into ecological champions, with an emphasis on outdoor learning, three nature playgrounds, fifteen California biomes, and water treatment strategies they can touch.

CONTEXT

Once a dump for bus parts and excavated soil, the ENC's suburban site a mile from the Pacific Ocean was painstakingly rehabbed throughout the '70s, '80s, and '90s into a biodiverse, forested "living laboratory" for nature education. Thirty years in, ENC enlisted LPA to design their first permanent building—an interpretive center providing hands-on education in ecological responsibility and sustainable practices. Ten years later, their campus vision was completed, with a preschool that seamlessly blends indoor and outdoor spaces to initiate a lifelong relationship with the environment.

OUTCOME

The net-positive ENC was the first LEED Platinum building in Orange County, and the preschool was the first Living Building Challenge Petal Certified building in Southern California. Under the shade of a butterfly-shaped roof, preschool students start each day in one of four outdoor classrooms. Three natural playgrounds use authentic materials for play structures. A nature walk exposes students to fifteen distinct California biomes. An organic garden teaches horticulture and healthy eating. On rainy days, stormwater rushes down rain chains as students track the flow from the roof to an on-site stream, collection basin, and then on to Newport Bay. With only natural ventilation in both buildings, designers used a mix of modeled and empirical data to size the second project's PV system, save money, and achieve 105% energy performance.

DESIGN FOR ENERGY

Operable windows, sliding glass walls, ceiling fans, and a sloped ceiling eliminated the need for a mechanical system, with PVs producing 105% of energy needs.

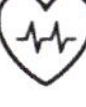

DESIGN FOR WELL-BEING

Human health and well-being is paramount, with organic gardens, a teaching kitchen, a shaded outdoor classroom, natural light and ventilation, and biophilia everywhere.

DESIGN FOR DISCOVERY

Measured performance of the net-positive interpretive center informed a new, hybrid approach to energy modeling for the preschool, right-sizing the PV array.

INTEGRATION

Meeting ENC's mission to inspire generations of ecological responsibility and sustainable practices required an approach that broke away from traditional practices. From the earliest planning stages, landscape architects, engineers, interior designers, and researchers worked with educators to rethink the facility's connections to nature and the community. The process started with the placement and orientation of both buildings. Taking cues from the sun, trees, and ocean, the visitor center and preschool were positioned north-south to capture maximum solar power. The landscape architects advocated to push the buildings as far north as possible to preserve mature palm and eucalyptus trees, while keeping shadows off solar panels. To minimize electrical loads, mechanical engineers proposed narrowing the preschool's footprint, allowing prevailing breezes from Newport Bay in the southwest to passively cool the building. Engineers and researchers studied wind patterns to help designers place operable windows on opposing sides of the buildings that channel cool air through an obstruction-free building and guide rising hot air along the sloped roofs. Landscape architects were involved in every planning meeting, blending indoor and outdoor spaces to support the educational programs and right-size the project to reduce the need for built space. They developed a tricycle path that winds through the site, connecting different learning zones activated with strategically placed boulders, logs, and tree stumps. A long slope running along the northern edge of the site was turned into a hill slide and climbing area.

"This project is an excellent example of how to apply the Framework for Design Excellence to a small space. This space is well integrated and serves a hugely impactful mission."

AIA CAE Jury

LANDSCAPE

RESEARCH ON ENVIRONMENTAL CONDITIONS CAUSED THE NATURE CENTER AND PRESCHOOL TO BE POSITIONED NORTH-SOUTH TO CAPTURE SUN EXPOSURE, PRESERVE TREES, AND IMPROVE CONNECTIONS TO NATURE.

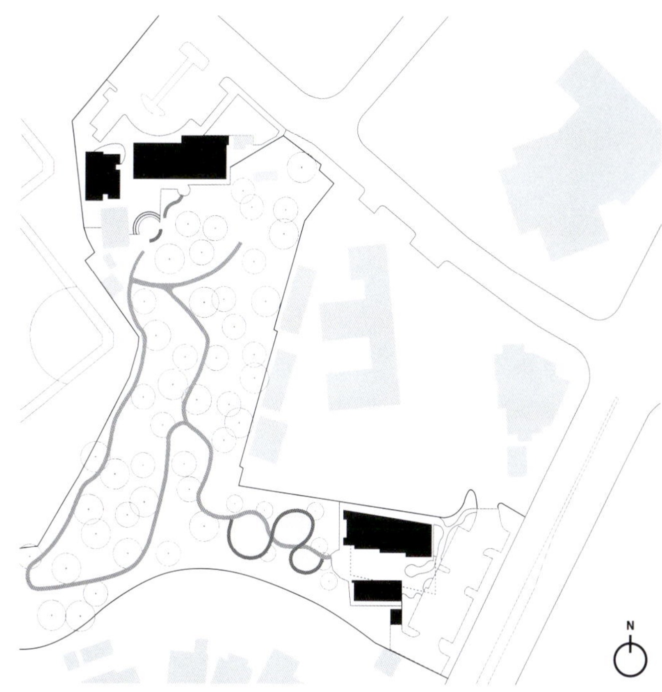

Performance

OPERATIONAL CARBON
EMISSIONS AVOIDED
(mT/year)

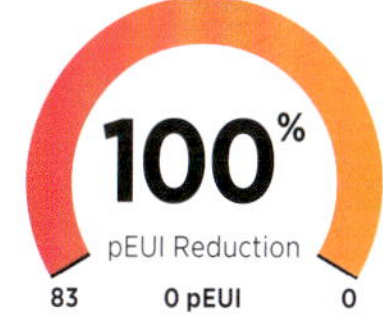

PREDICTED ENERGY
USE INTENSITY
(kBtu/sf/year)

Met the AIA Commitment
70% THRESHOLD
at the time of design

Project	K-12 | Nonprofit | 2008, 2019
Budget	$8M
Scale	Small | 19,380 sf

Impact

100% of Spaces Have Natural Ventilation

100% of Spaces Have Daylight Autonomy

100% Native Plantings

Recognition

COTE Top Ten Plus AIA National, 2020
Award of Excellence AIA/CAE, 2021
Living Building Petal ENC Preschool
2 LEED Platinum

enc

LOOKING FORWARD

VALLEY COLLEGE
MONARCHS

A MODEL FOR THE FUTURE PRACTICE

Michelle Amt **FAIA**
2024 Chair, AIA Committee on the Environment (COTE)

Most of us now know that buildings are responsible for more than 40 percent of annual global carbon emissions; what many might not know is that by 2060, global building floor area is expected to double. The massive change needed to reduce global carbon emissions during this period of huge construction growth is unprecedented and urgent.

As an industry, we can no longer ignore the importance of portfolio-wide decarbonization and changing how we approach the challenge. We must practice differently and think differently. We can't settle for small steps forward if we expect to achieve a net-zero future.

In this book, LPA has shown us what "no excuses" means. They have consistently achieved ambitious performance goals across a broad portfolio of projects. Time and time again, LPA has demonstrated how sustainability and building performance can be applied broadly to everyday building types. They've delivered exceptional results regardless of client ambitions, budgetary constraints, regulatory environments, and market forces.

As we look to the future, their progress has charted a path that every designer must take: cutting emissions on every project, for every budget, at every scale. To achieve results, LPA has developed a new model of practice, one that successfully harnesses the full power of an integrated design firm. They bring disciplines together as partners, establishing performance expectations, creating resources, and conducting research to inform data-driven design, while cultivating a culture of accountability and shared responsibility.

There is nothing magical in this approach. No secret sauce. They built sustainability into the firm's DNA and then backed it up by giving teams the tools and resources to pursue their goals. They didn't set out to blaze new trails; they worked to get better. Step by step, they developed their process and culture. They learned that education and a spirit of accountability are essential. Clients are viewed as partners, recognizing that the only way forward is to meet the realities of budget and policy.

The projects highlighted in this book illustrate the influence we can have as architects, designers, and engineers, working as a unit. On the TIDE Academy, you see all disciplines collaborating to create a public school on a limited site that will inspire generations of learners. The Edwards Lifesciences campus is an example of a decades-long relationship between designers and a client focused on merging sustainability with the workplace goals of a company developing lifesaving technologies.

Exploring LPA's work, over and over again you see an iterative process backed by research and community engagement producing unexpected, amazing results. Their focus on sustainability and building performance was not at the expense of notable architecture; they design places that inspire learning, foster community, and empower people.

LPA's work shows us what is possible. We can make cutting carbon emissions and improved building performance the foundation of good design, while creating meaningful experiences, grounded in their unique place, that support thriving communities at all scales.

When you hear LPA leaders talk about their mission and culture, you realize we can do better. In their practice, approach, and commitment, they demonstrate a different way of working, a spirit of inclusiveness and rigor that will be essential for tackling the challenges ahead. They present us with the future of practice: mission-driven, interdisciplinary, and relentless in the pursuit of excellence, for this and future generations.

BUILDING A CULTURE OF SHARED RESPONSIBILITY

We've been evolving what it means to practice as an integrated design firm for three decades. Our work illustrates that a collaborative, inclusive design approach can produce results. What's next? Five LPA leaders—each from a different discipline—discuss the cultivation of the culture that will confront the challenges ahead.

Kari Kikuta **PLA, ASLA**
Director of Landscape Architecture

Bryan Seamer **SE, LEED GA**
Director of Structural Engineering

Kate Mraw **RID, CID, ALEP, LEED AP**
Director of K-12

Ozzie Tapia **AIA, LEED AP**
Design Director

Erik Ring **PE, LEED FELLOW**
Director of Engineering

WHAT MAKES LPA'S INTEGRATED CULTURE DIFFERENT THAN OTHER FIRMS?

Bryan Seamer *(Director of Structural Engineering)*: To me it's one word: trust. We invest in our culture, the ability to bring together people with different expertise, who may in some cases conflict with each other, to find the best design decisions for a project. Our culture creates a condition where we trust each other. We feel we can push back on ideas. We can express our own perspectives without fear of a relationship being damaged.

Ozzie Tapia *(Design Director)*: We don't care where the ideas come from. We really do check our egos at the door. Ultimately, what makes us successful and what makes our process really work is that together we come up with an idea that makes that project better for our clients.

Kari Kikuta *(Director of Landscape Architecture)*: At the end of the day, we're having really difficult conversations. It's those kinds of conversations that drive our disciplines to do better across the board. Architecture, interiors, landscape—we all want to perform at a higher level together.

Erik Ring *(Director of Engineering)*: All of us recognize that as individuals we have a certain expertise, a certain perspective that's really important to the project, but it's incomplete. We recognize that great design is shared authorship between a lot of different experts and our clients to deliver a far better project than any one designer could on their own.

Kate Mraw *(Director of K-12)*: We're really talking about being on the same side of the table as each other, facing that problem together with high emotional intelligence, and knowing how to deal with conflict resolution. We always want to be able to say, "I'm not the smartest person in the room on this topic, but I'm going to make sure that the smartest person on this topic *is* in the room."

Bryan: It's quite intentional, too. We've worked to seed our culture with these values. One of the key things, I think, is how it began. We didn't become an integrated firm to capture more fees. It wasn't a business decision. It began because we felt we needed to do it to design better-performing buildings. And that has driven the development of our culture.

HOW DO YOU CREATE A CULTURE OF SHARED RESPONSIBILITY?

Kate: We win together, and we lose together.

Erik: That's really true. We measure our success as teams, not as individuals or individual disciplines. Even at a company level, we focus on the overall health and success of our company. We have a culture where if any part of our company is succeeding, we all celebrate in that. We celebrate together; we work on fixing problems together.

Bryan: When I worked as a consulting engineer, it was always about designing a building or a site. I would see a project as "Okay, I need a high bay with a fifty-foot span over here, and the column grid will look like this." Now we're designing spaces for people. I see a project and it's about a community that's been underserved, a neighborhood that needs recreation spaces, people who need access to health services. We start our projects talking about the people who are going to benefit from the project.

Kari: And that perspective is shared through the entire team. When we kick off a project, the design concept is shared out to the team, not just the design leads. It's not led by a particular discipline. That attitude resonates through the duration of the project—the team is working on the whole project.

Ozzie: It's not just the architect pushing or pulling everybody along. The entire team has skin in the game. They believe that what they're doing is the best thing for that project.

Kate: Shared responsibility also means a shared understanding of the vision. We build on that together and need to constantly be learning. Shared responsibility is about everybody understanding our goals and the steps we need to take to create healthier, inspiring environments.

Kari: We often hire people coming from a landscape-only or an architectural-only or an engineering-only firm who aren't used to integrated, collaborative discussions. We need to spend time to get them accustomed to this type of dialogue and have them feel comfortable pushing back or really digging in and taking on that responsibility.

Bryan: It takes a real definitive decision for a landscape architect or engineer to join a firm like LPA. We need to peel back the layers of misconception they have about working this way, because many of them have spent their whole career working in a system where that mutual respect doesn't exist. We have to break that down.

WHAT WILL IT TAKE FOR THE INDUSTRY TO REACH OUR CARBON-REDUCTION GOALS?

Ozzie: There must be an awareness that every action has a reaction. Every material that you are selecting has a carbon footprint. That level of understanding and awareness is important for every decision that we make.

Bryan: "No excuses" is a mindset. You can always find a reason to take the easy path, the path of least resistance. You have to have a mindset that "I'm going to lean into this." We embed this in our teams, this attitude, to put performance at the forefront of every project.

Erik: I never want to be the designer who's designing a building that can't even survive a generation. These are hard, complex problems that we collectively are being tasked to address. But that's also what makes it fun to come to work every day, working with great people to try to take on these really, really hard problems.

INTEGRATED DESIGN FOR A SUSTAINABLE FUTURE

Keith Hempel **FAIA**
President, CDO

Wendy Rogers **FAIA**
CEO, CTO

Designers, by nature, are forward thinkers. We don't see what is; we see what could be. Looking forward is inherent to our process, yet daunting in a fast-changing world. It is our job to recognize the significance of the challenge ahead, embrace it, and take it on with a commitment to innovation and elevating the communities we serve.

As a firm, we believe we have a professional responsibility to eliminate carbon emissions from the projects we design. And we need to get there while fulfilling our clients' vision and working within the realities of budgets, codes, typology, geology, and whatever else is thrown in our paths.

Both of us have spent our entire careers at LPA. We were mentored by passionate designers who made sustainability part of our DNA and constantly pushed us to do better. They refused to accept the status quo. Our clients rarely came to us with performance goals in mind. We saw it as our job to demonstrate that we can create meaningful places that support the environment and people, while still meeting our clients' business goals.

We've come a long way. We've survived economic crashes, a pandemic, and untold natural and man-made disasters. At each step, we were able to come together and find our path, maintaining our independence and values. We have emerged as "a collective of designers, free spirits, innovators, and

explorers" who are rallying around shared values and a shared responsibility to make a difference in our communities.

The next steps—the leaps we will need to make as an industry—won't be easy. The decarbonization of our work will be the biggest test we will face in our careers. Throughout the industry, it's inspiring to see talent and resources mobilizing to confront the issues. Alliances are forming. We're doing a better job of tracking materials, setting standards, and creating tools.

Yet, we know it's not enough. We're not going to fulfill our ambitions unless we fundamentally work differently, think differently. For too long, architects, engineers, landscape architects, and designers have settled for working in their lanes. To go to the next level—creating regenerative, healthy projects that give more than they take—we need to push beyond the old boundaries to create a culture that values every idea and voice.

There are many opportunities ahead. Our approach to an aging generation of buildings can be a paradigm shift for the profession, driving a new generation of creativity and innovation. New materials will change how we build and think about structure. Technology is driving efficiency and freeing designers to reach for new heights.

But we're not going to get there if so many in our industry continue to work in the same fashion, settling for business as usual. It's too easy to dismiss the targets or throw up your hands at project constraints. Our commitment to eliminate carbon from projects should unite us and align disciplines and designers in a common cause. The task is too big to do alone. It requires partnerships, innovation, and a shared belief that our work is always better when everyone sits at the table as equals.

This book is our offer of proof that the integration of disciplines is essential for progress. We achieve what we do by bringing together disparate groups of talent and expertise around common goals. It doesn't matter if an engineer or designer is in-house or a consultant. The culture of inclusion, collaboration, and shared mission is the essential ingredient in every project.

In our work, we try to show that it is possible to improve, to come together as a firm to make a difference. Any firm can do it. Invest in education. Set goals. Let research and community voices guide the process. Empower designers to incorporate performance, wellness, experience, and community into the design process for every project, and encourage them to set high goals. We didn't start off hitting our targets—we worked at our process and committed to a culture of learning and constant improvement, seeking out ways to practice differently and do better.

Going forward, our commitment to sustainability and applied research must be unwavering. We can't wall ourselves off from new ideas and different ways of working. We must remain agile and listen to our clients and communities. We won't solve every problem. But finding answers is what we do. We can be the leaders, the facilitators, to bring people together to create inspirational, healthy places.

It's our time as designers—designers of all disciplines—to step up and meet the moment. We must be bold and refuse to accept the norm. We can't take the easy way out. We have a responsibility to our communities and future generations to remain focused on our carbon targets and leave the world a better place than we found it.

No excuses.

WE BELIEVE

Everything counts.

There is always a way.

We don't do this alone.

APPENDIX

Awards / Recognition

The recognition of the 2025 AIA Architecture Firm Award is testimony to the commitment we made long ago that a process focused on design excellence and high performance creates value for our clients, the environment, and our society at large.

AIA (AMERICAN INSTITUTE OF ARCHITECTS) NATIONAL AWARDS

AIA Architecture Firm Award

LPA Design Studios, 2025

AIA Architecture Award

TIDE Academy, 2023

AIA/COTE Top Ten Plus

Environmental Nature Center and Preschool, 2020

AIA/CAE

Lanier High School, 2024

TIDE Academy, 2022

ENC Preschool, 2021

Tarbut V'Torah Community Day School Expansion, 2020

e3 Civic High School, 2015

Coastline Community College, Newport Beach Campus, 2014

CSU Northridge, Student Recreation Center, 2013

Santiago Canyon College, Learning Resource Center, 2008

AIA/CAE/SCUP

Riverside CCD Center for Social Justice and Civil Liberties, 2014

CSU Northridge, Student Recreation Center, 2014

Santiago Canyon College, Learning Resource Center, 2007

AIA Faith & Form Award

Christ Cathedral Arboretum and Tower of Hope, 2018

AIA/CEFPI Shirley Cooper Award

Environmental Nature Center, 2008

NATIONAL RECOGNITION

AISC: American Institute of Steel Construction

Los Angeles Valley College Monarch Center, IDEAS Award, 2016

Spectrum IV, IDEAS Award, 2019

ASLA: American Society of Landscape Architects

Toyota South Campus Expansion, Honor, 2005

IESNA: Illuminating Engineering Society of North America

Agnew K-12 Campus, Award of Merit, 2024

TIDE Academy, Outdoor Lighting Design Award of Merit, 2023

TIDE Academy, Interior Lighting Design Award of Merit, 2023

Crown Valley Community Center, Environmental Design Award of Merit, 2021

Eastvale STEM Academy, Interior Award of Merit, 2021

Spectrum IV, Award of Merit, 2019

701B Street, Award of Merit, 2019

Mazda North America HQ, Interior Award of Merit, 2018

Mazda North America HQ, Environmental Design Award of Merit, 2018

Edwards Starr Atrium, Interior Award of Merit, 2018

San Diego Trolley Station, Energy / Environment Award of Merit, 2015

San Diego Trolley Station, Exterior Award of Merit, 2015

Pan Pacific Mechanical, Interior Award of Merit, 2015

Coastline Community College, Newport Beach Campus, Energy Award of Merit, 2014

LPA San Jose Office, Interior Award of Merit, 2014

NCSEA: National Council of Structural Engineers Associations

West Hollywood Park Recreation & Aquatic Center, Structural Engineering Excellence, 2023

UC San Diego York Hall Seismic Retrofit, Structural Engineering Excellence, 2023

Cal Poly Pomona Student Rec Center, Excellence in Structural Engineering Award, 2017

Tower of Hope, Award of Excellence—Renovation, Retrofit, Alteration, 2016

Visit the landing page:
AIA ARCHITECTURE
FIRM AWARD

AIA COMPONENT COTE AND HONOR AWARDS 2014–2024

COTE AWARD

AIA Orange County

Wimberley Village Library, 2024

RiverRock Headquarters, 2023

Edwards Expansion, 2022

WeHo Park & Aquatic Center, 2022

Palomar College Humanities, 2021

Edwards Lifesciences Starr Atrium, 2017

3250 Olcott, 2017

CSU East Bay, Support Center, 2017

Los Angeles Valley College Monarch Student Center, 2016

Montgomery Middle School, 2014

AIA Long Beach / South Bay

LPA Irvine Studio, 2021

AIA San Antonio

LPA San Antonio Studio, 2020

AIA Los Angeles

West Hollywood AVRS, 2018

AIA San Diego

LPA San Diego Studio, 2016

e3 Civic High School, 2014

AIA Pasadena Foothill

Cal Poly Pomona Student Rec Center, 2015

HONOR AWARD

AIA Orange County

Wimberley Village Library, 2024

College of the Desert Library, 2024

CSUSB Student Union, 2023

Palomar College Humanities, 2021

Normandie Supportive Housing, 2020

Environmental Nature Center Preschool, 2020

TVT Community Day School Expansion, 2020

Riverside CCD Coil School of the Arts, 2018

Edwards Lifesciences, Starr Atrium, 2017

West Hollywood AVRS, 2016

AIA California / CASH

Eastvale STEM Academy, 2021

Encinitas USD Facilities Master Plan, 2021

Agnew High School, 2019

Hugo Reid Elementary School, 2019

Fremont High School, 2018

Monarch High School, 2018

TIDE Academy, 2017

Johnson Middle School, 2016

San Marcos High School, 2015

e3 Civic High School, 2015

Paramount High School, 2014

Irvine Unified School District, 2014

AIA Silicon Valley

Piedmont Hills High School, 2020

AIA Inland California

CSU San Bernardino Center for Global Innovation, 2020

Riverside CCD Culinary Arts Academy, 2020

AIA Central Valley

Piedmont Hills High School, 2019

West Valley College, Cilker Center, 2017

AIA Long Beach / South Bay

El Camino College Math, Business and Science, 2015

AIA San Diego

Palomar College Humanities, 2015

LPA San Jose Studio, 2014

LANDSCAPE AND ENGINEERING HONOR AWARDS 2013–2024

ASLA: AMERICAN SOCIETY OF LANDSCAPE ARCHITECTS

ASLA Southern California

ENC & Preschool, 2021

TVT Community Day School, 2018

CSU Northridge Wellness Center, 2016

ASLA San Diego

Grape Day Park, 2024

ASLA Sierra

Towers @ 2nd, 2018

College of San Mateo, 2016

Lincoln High School, 2016

ASLA Texas

ENC & Preschool, 2021

Pleasanton ES, 2019

SEA: STRUCTURAL ENGINEERS ASSOCIATIONS

SEAOC

UCSD York Hall Seismic Rehabilitation, Excellence Award for Retrofit, 2023

9625 Towne Centre Drive, Excellence Award, 2021

Tower of Hope, Excellence Award, 2016

SEAOSC

Cal Poly Pomona Student Rec Center, Excellence Award, 2016

Tower of Hope, Excellence Award, 2016

CSU Northridge Student Recreation Center, Excellence Award, 2015

SEAOSD

Grossmont College Performing Arts Center, Excellence Award, 2024

UCSD York Hall Seismic Rehabilitation, Excellence Award, 2023

Palomar College Learning Resource Center, Excellence Award, 2022

9625 Towne Centre Drive, Excellence Award, 2021

ASCE: AMERICAN SOCIETY OF CIVIL ENGINEERS

ASCE Los Angeles Section

Villa Park High School Science Center, Civil Sustainability Project of the Year, 2023

Cypress College SEM, Outstanding Structural Engineering Project of the Year, 2022

Edwards Lifesciences Starr Atrium, Structural Project of the Year, 2021

Tower of Hope, Outstanding Historic Renovation Project, 2017

West Hollywood AVRS, Architectural Engineering Project of the Year, 2016

Coastline Community College, Newport Beach Campus, Sustainability Project of the Year, 2013

ASCE Los Angeles Metro Branch

West Hollywood AVRS, Outstanding Innovation Project of the Year, 2016

ASCE Orange County Branch

Glaukos Corporation Collegial Office Project, Civil Sustainable Engineering Project Award, 2024

Villa Park High School Science Center, Outstanding Civil Sustainable Project of the Year, 2023

Vans Headquarters, Civil Sustainability Project of the Year, 2022

Cypress College Science, Engineering & Math, Structural Project of the Year, 2022

Palomar College Learning Resource Center, Structural Excellence Award, 2022

Edwards Lifesciences Starr Atrium, Structural Project of the Year, 2021

Crown Valley Park, Civil Outstanding Land Development Project, 2020

County of Orange Building 16, Structural Project of the Year, 2020

ENC Preschool, Civil Sustainability Project of the Year, 2020

Tarbut V'Torah Community Day School Expansion, Civil Sustainability Project of the Year, 2019

Rancho Mission Viejo Pavilion, Civil Community Improvement Project of the Year, 2019

Great Park Ice Complex, Structural Project of the Year, 2019

Tower of Hope, Outstanding Historic Renovation Project, 2017

Park Place, Land Development Project of the Year, 2015

ASCE Sacramento Section

Hall Memorial Park, Civil Parks and Recreation Project of the Year, 2020

ASCE Region 9 California

West Hollywood AVRS, Architectural Engineering Project of the Year, 2016

Coastline Community College, Newport Beach Campus, Architectural Engineering Project of the Year, 2013

Acknowledgments

We don't do this alone. We are grateful to our clients, collaborators, and colleagues who have challenged and supported the evolution of our firm. Our journey over the last sixty years reflects the work of untold people over the decades who have come together to create a collaborative culture based in humility and a commitment to a sustainable future. We are inspired by industry leaders like Ed Mazria and Michelle Amt, whose words grace this book. They constantly remind us there is still much work to do and the time to act is now.

The concept for this book started as a way to celebrate our sixtieth anniversary and the influence of our former president, Dan Heinfeld, who retired in 2023 after forty-five years of visionary leadership. Books are no different from projects—much is learned on the iterative path of reflection and discovery. In this case, the confluence of the book and our AIA Firm Award submission brought clarity to our story and message. For both, we sought to demonstrate that there is always a way to create a high-performing project, regardless of budget or scale.

We are indebted to the collective talents of the principals; associates; architects; landscape architects; structural, mechanical, electrical, and civil engineers; plumbing, lighting and interior designers; planners; researchers and the firm disciplines -- accounting, contracts, human resources, marketing, inspire design, quality and practice management. It is this ecosystem of 530 dedicated people at LPA who understand everything counts that enables us to balance our brand, business, and culture to deliver exceptional projects with our clients.

Special thanks go to our internal "book team" from our leadership group: Ozzie Tapia, Kate Mraw, Kari Kikuta, Helen Pierce, and Erik Ring, who went the extra mile to share perspective and project stories. Also, thanks to Apoorva Pradhan, Eddy Lopez, and Kyle Griffin, who retrieved the data, created the graphics, and supported the team throughout the project.

We applaud the efforts of our creative director, Ron Leland, who diligently led the process, and the brilliance of Kevin Brass, who found our voice and wrote the stories with Daniel Scheuerman. Melanie Giacalone brought her exceptional graphic skills to each carefully crafted page, collaborating with our communications team, Carl Hyndman, Mike Gembarski, Patrick Campbell, Sierra Runnels, and Sarah Pratt.

We deeply appreciate the wisdom and friendship of Ken Sanders, whose guidance has helped shape our vision, and we are grateful for the friendship of our colleague Tim Culvahouse and the work we've done together over the decades. Tim introduced us to Karen Robichaud, who deserves special thanks for being an energetic coach over the last year, bringing vitality and clarity to the editorial process as we refined our message. We are a collaborative group who truly believe in every voice at the table. Karen's unrelenting patience, listening to every point of view, keenly guided us to share our no-excuses mindset. We would also be remiss if we didn't recognize the tireless commitment of Betsy del Monte, whose voice and meticulous editing authored the video for our firm award and influenced the tone of our book. We are thankful and appreciative of their wisdom.

Our work is brought to life in this book by many talented photographers, who have beautifully captured the essence of our projects and kindly shared them. We were fortunate to work with Gordon Goff at ORO Editions in the creation of this book.

Putting together ***No Excuses*** has been an exploration of our collective beliefs and our commitment to design a firm that will confront climate change. Our goal was to share a story that demonstrates what a firm of any size can accomplish if they simply stop making excuses and focus on performance.

Wendy Rogers and Keith Hempel, February 2025

Firm Profile

LPA is a multidisciplinary integrated design collective united by a shared responsibility to deliver high-performance design on every project, for every budget and scale. Our culture focuses on removing barriers between disciplines to ensure every voice is heard, all input is valued. We are committed to delivering timeless, sustainable projects that benefit the environment, generate lasting value, and enrich the human experience.

Throughout our history, LPA has taken a leadership role in promoting energy efficiency and sustainability, setting new benchmarks for what defines a great project. Our goal is to find continual improvement in our work and develop a model for a design process that builds consensus, finds innovation, and does more with less.

LPADesignStudios.com

LPA Team Members

Faisal Aboud
Chris Aeria
Perla Aguayo
Anthony Aguilar
Carlyle Aguilar
Sasha Aguilera
Xavier Aguon
Chris Alcala
Brianna Alexander
Brittany Allen
Ella Altaji
Maya Amyx
Kylar Anderson
Laura Jeanne Andrews
Chloe Andruss
Kelly Angell
Roman Antonio
Eric Araiza
Nick Arambarri
Justin Argomaniz
Roland Argomaniz
Emily Aschbrenner
Bradley Atnip
Stacy Auslam
Kayla Ayala
Niko Babic
Mitch Bacon
Aldo Bacuzzi
Lauren Ballard
Mariana Ballina
Winston Bao
Maritza Barajas

Jonathan Bassett
Manidipa Basu
Eric Baumgartner
Daniel Bayer
Yashar Behtoteh
Vlad Beljic
David Beller
Rohit Belsare
Kevin Bendtsen
Cameron Best
Tiffiny Betancourt
Rosemarie Bettencourt
Brenda Beza
Rich Bienvenu
Sevan Biran-Shalom
Greg Bistritz
April Blackburn
Erin Blankenau
Josh Borad
Frederick Braggs
Kevin Brass
Ben Bravo
Ifrane Brennan
Carrie Bridge
Wil Briones
Franco Brown
Ridvan Bruss
Katie Cavazos Budzinski
Karla Burlaza
Dave Burt
Monica Bustos
Cora Butler

Tessa Cain
Patrick Campbell
Maddi Carey
Nick Casolari
Kevin Castillo
Kimberly Castillo
Jessica Castro
Federico Cavazos
Becky Ceballos
Nicole Chaco
Jomay Liao Chan
Melissa Chandler
Casey Chapin
Oscar Chavez
Derek Chen
Mohan Cheng
Kitty Cheung
Angela Chiang
Lawrence Chiu
Shih-Chia Chiu
Kevin Cho
Daniel Chong
Andrew Christiansen
Elizabeth Christensen
Danielle Cleveland
Michelle Cobb
Alejandra Colina
Chase Collins
Noah Colome
Kevin Concolino
Carlos Constantino
Bill Cooke

Brandee Corrales Lopez
John Courtney
Tessa Couvrette
Anne Criddle
Juliet Crowder
Jordan Currier
Wendy Dailey
Rick D'Amato
Peter Damore
Rakhi Dasgupta
Brian Daugherty
Derek Davis
Michael Davis
Sierra Davis
Daniel Day
Brandon de Arakal
Paula de Farro
Loryelle De La Pena
Alison De La Torre
Nathan Dea
Fawn Deason
Bill Debevc
Lindsay DeCeault
Jillian Deneroff
Laura Diamante
Amy DiCosola
LaDonna Dimas
Fang Ding
Tom Do
Amber Donaldson
Craig Drone
Sonaly Dudheker

Anna Duffy
Tim Duffy
Joe Dunn
Cindy Dunnells
Damon Dusterhoft
Dave Eaves
Elaina Echevarria
Chad Edgley
Kat Esselstrom
Walter Estay
Maryam Fakhar Sabet
Alexa Feldman
Nicole Fennell
Erik Fernandez
Kelly Ferris
Radu Filimon
Steve Flanagan
Denise Flatley
Holden Fleck
April Flores
Sara Flowers
Shae Foster
Juliette Fournier
Brad Fowers
Deb Fox
Amber Freeman
Mia Frietze
Rita Frink
Alfred Froberg
Laurence Garcia
Maribel Garcia Abrica
Morgan Gargas

Jeffrey Gauthier
Mike Gembarski
Rocio Gertler
Antolin Gervacio
Melanie Giacalone
Jake Gillespie
Alex Gilmore
Dave Gilmore
Sevanna Gilpin
Pegah Giovannetti
Ronnie Gomez
Michael Gonzaguirre
Ron Gonzales
Alan Gonzalez
Gabriela Gonzalez
Oscar Gonzalez
Samantha Gonzalez
Rodrigo Gorgazzi
Bodhi Goswami
Jacob Gottlieb
Beto Granados
Katie Gray
Ken Green
Kyle Griffin
Sarah Grondona
Aldo Guerra
Hector Guerra Garza
Nathan Guisande
Darcie Gumbayan
Ceci Gutierrez
Sophia Ha
Brittany Haberstroh-Baker

Ben Hamilton
Andrew Han
Hosuk Han
Mark Harmon
Amber Haro
Onjelica Harris
Morgan Harrison
Jeremy Hart
Sherry Hart
Lindsay Hayward
Cassie Heminway
Keith Hempel
Raul Hernandez
Leo Hernandez Macias
Jose Hernandez Ocampo
Philip Herzer
Adrienne High
Alejandra Hinojosa
John Hoenig
Erik Holliday
Jessie Hong
Lindy Hsieh
Christian Huber
Kenya Huezo
Lance Hunter
Long Huynh
Carl Hyndman
Jessica Isler
Kim Izadi
Lizzy Jaime
Cassidy Janes
Rodrigo Jaramillo

Rowena Jayamanne
Briseida Jimenez
D. Alex John
Andrew Johnson
Jennifer Johnson
Eric Jones
Jake Junge
Shima Kaheh
Lindsay Kalyvas
Matthew Kanamori
Brynnan Kaufmann
Gurneet Kaur
Veli Kemal
Steve Key
Vidula Khadilkar
Kari Kikuta
Alice Kim
Chanhoo Kim
Hyeran Kim
Jay Kim
Jeanie Kim
Julia Kirk
Jared Klingsporn
Lauren Kobes
Emily Koch
Travis Koss
Alexis Kotzambasis
Jill Kramer
Nick Kramer
Miles Kushin
Maria LaFever

LPA Team Members

Albert Lam
Natasha Landicho
Angelica Larios
Leah Larson
Clare Lassus
Steve Lathus
Karis Lawson
Amanda Layman
Tan Le
Curtis Lechner
Alyssa Lee
Jonathan Lee
Terri Lee
Amber Leenheer
Ron Leland
Chris Lentz
Kevin Leslie
Adrian Leung
Bing Li
Jack Li
Leo Li
Muhsin Lihony
Sam Lim
Jordan Lin
Corrie Lindsay
Kate Littlejohn
Genevie Livingston
Luis Llanos
Alejandro Lopez
Eddy Lopez
Elena Lopez
Henry Lopez
Megan Lovejoy
Victoria Lowell
Wilson Lu
Lauren Lugliani
Carmelle Luminarias
Scott Lux
Nick Ma
Patti MacKenzie
Maria Madrigal
Ruth Malkin
Isabel Mandujano Aguilar
Jordanah Marcelo
Elijah Marcum
Liliana Marquez Trujillo
Douglas Marquis
Mills Martin
Stephanie Matsuda-Strand
Roy Mathew
Theresa Maurer
Travis McCarty Garcia
Corey McClaine
Patrick McClintock
Kanika McDougall
Kelsey McDowell
Maureen McShane
Memo Medina
Nicole Mehta
Bianca Melgazo
Sy Melgazo
Adam Melius
Denise Mendelssohn
Faby Mendez
Amanda Menschel
Michael Michalek
Yvonne Miller
Jon Mills
Young Min
Levy Minemann
Ellen Mitchell
Daniel Molina
Andrea Montejano
Gerardo Montes Martinez
Tanner Moore
Kate Mraw
Emma Muresan
Devin Murphy
Jill Murray
Rick Musto
Sang Nam
Rachel Nasland
Anna Nasonova
Carly Nathanson
Alex Negulescu
Kristy Nelson
Laura Nelson
Ben Ness
Anna New
Justen Newby
Morgan Newman
Tony Nguyen
Vincent Nguyen
Katie Nilmeier
Naomi Nishimoto
Mike Norouzi
Jose Nunez Areyan
Kyle O'Connor
Miray Oktem Tunali
Stan Olsiewski
Hannah Oppelt
Jim Oppelt
Angie Ortiz
Katharine Owens
Jen Ozai
Elli Pace
Leah Padden
Carlo Pane
Micah Pang
Nimesh Parikh
Steven Park
Lika Pasurishvili
Kelly Pavey
Brita Pearson
Jill Pedro
Ha Pham
Phillip Pham
Kimari Phillips
Bill Pickford
Helen Pierce
Roodza Pierrelus
Andy Pippin
Jared Plummer
Samantha Pohler

Steve Pomerenke
Matthew Porreca
Ethan Powell
Tracey Powl
Apoorva Pradhan
Harshda Prasad
Magda Prendergast
Karl Prinz
Erick Pulido
Erika Pulido
Michael Puno
Jichun Qin
Maria Quintero
Connell Railey
Wen Raymundo
Kyle Rebector
Valeria Redekosky
Francesca Redetzke
Kelsea Regier
Angelo Ricasata
Robert Richardson
Erik Ring
Andrea Rocha Ponce
Ester Rodriguez
Maria Rodriguez
Teresa Rodriguez
Wendy Rogers
Ben Rosas
Kristen Royer
Lauren Rudd
Sierra Runnells

Erin Runyon
Beth Russell
Luca Scarpello
Krista Scheib
Daniel Scheuerman
Greg Schneekluth
Doug Seamark
Bryan Seamer
Chris Senviel
Mary Seufert
Sonal Shah
Huda Shahid
Bylasan Shalabi
Kathereen Shinkai
Craig Shulman
Ginger Shulman
Chris Shyy
Josh Sienkiewicz
Carla Simental
Jennifer Simmons
Sylvia Situ
Matt Sloss
Krista Smallwood
Michelyn Smith
Brian So
Lydia Solomon
Wil Soriano
Amalia Sosa Ramirez
Daniel Stone
Riley Summer
Sam Sun

Danah Sundberg
Lam Ta
Melody Tang
Heather Tapia
Ozzie Tapia
Vahid Tavakoulnia
Arsalan Tavassoli
Kandis Teague
AJ Tezveren-Johnson
Ti Than
John Thao
Kate Thomas
Chris Tindall
Steve Tiner
Anh-Thy Tobin
Menard Torculas
Emily Torres
Tiffany Torres
Frank Tran
Tin Tran
Queysha Trimble
Carlos Trujillo
Anthony Tsui
Sophia Ulloa
Zoe Van Duffelen
Ashley Van Kirk
Kelli Van Stone
Shalin Varghese
Natalee Velazquez
Edgar Villa
Lindsay Votel

Mandy Vu
Ekta Wali
Keeley Wandrocke
Daniel Wang
Esther Wang
Tony Wang
Megan Ward
Sarah Ward
Julian Watt
Greg Webb
Meagan Whitton-Garcia
Andrew Wickham
Charlie Williams
Fallon Williams
John Wilson
Matt Winter
Jim Wirick
Suzanne Wong
Juliana Woo
Jeff Yamamoto
Ger Yang
Jane Yang
Jane Yoon
Inno Yoro
Jane You
Elisa Younger
Mansour Yousefpour
Carlos Zepeda Velazquez
Alissa Zhu
Hormoz Ziaebrahimi
Natalie Zweig-Chewning

Photography Credits

Banner Mountain Media
Grass Valley, CA

Jason Boulanger
Jason Boulanger Photography
East Bernstadt, KY

Cristian Costea
Costea Photography, Inc
Newport Beach, CA

Bruce Damonte
Bruce Damonte Architectural Photography
San Francisco, CA

Sean Gallagher
Sean G Photos
Dallas, TX

Carl Hyndman
LPA Design Studios
Irvine, CA

Nick Merrick
Hall+Merrick+McCaugherty
Chicago, IL

Matthew Niemann
Matthew Niemann Photography
San Antonio, TX

Jason O'Rear
Jason O'Rear Photography
San Francisco, CA

RMA Architectural Photography
Irvine, CA

Jun Tang
Jun Tang Photography
Irvine, CA

Bill Thompson
Pencilbox Studios
Corona, CA

ORO Editions
Publishers of Architecture, Art, and Design
Gordon Goff: Publisher

www.oroeditions.com
info@oroeditions.com

Published by ORO Editions

Foreword: Ed Mazria
Contributors: Michelle Amt, Dan Heinfeld, Keith Hempel, Wendy Rogers
Author: LPA Design Studios
Book Design: LPA Design Studios
Project Manager: Jake Anderson

10 9 8 7 6 5 4 3 2 1 First Edition

ISBN: 978-1-957183-76-3

Prepress and Print Work by ORO Editions Inc.
Printed in China

ORO Editions makes a continuous effort to minimize the overall carbon footprint of its publications. As part of this goal, ORO, in association with Global ReLeaf, arranges to plant trees to replace those used in the manufacturing of the paper produced for its books. Global ReLeaf is an international campaign run by American Forests, one of the world's oldest nonprofit conservation organizations. Global ReLeaf is American Forests' education and action program that helps individuals, organizations, agencies, and corporations improve the local and global environment by planting and caring for trees.